PEACE CORPS SYNDROME

Memoirs and Letters
Of A Peace Corps Volunteer
To Brazil
1966-1968

RON HORTON

Happenstance Books

Beaver, Arkansas

2007

Published by Happenstance Books
PO Box 28
Beaver, AR 72613-0028
Happenstancebooks.com

Cover Design by Penguin Graphics II

Copyright © 2007 by Ronald T. Horton

All rights reserved. No part of this book may be used or reproduced by any means: graphic, electronic, or mechanical, including photocopying, recording, taping or by any information storage retrieval system without the written permission of the author, except in the case of brief quotations embodied in critical articles and reviews.

Printed in the United States of America

First Edition   2007

ISBN 0-9786366-2-7

Library of Congress Control Number 2007930176

To my precious mother, Elsie Horton, for saving all one hundred of my letters home from Peace Corps. To my darling wife, Sharon Freeman Horton, my psychic twin and love of my life, for editing my memoirs and putting up with me. To the once-in-a-life-time Peace Corps camaraderie, a magical concoction of great and altruistic characters. To Rob, who saved me from Viet Nam, and to the inherently sweet and good hearted nature of the Brazilian people. My love and blessings to you all. And to all of you who realize the great danger we all face from corporatism + authoritarian government = Fascism.

Preface

When President John F. Kennedy gave his famous speech, "Ask not what your country can do for you - ask what you can do for your country," I had no chance against such a blatant request and joined Peace Corps in 1966. During my two years in Jungle Hospitals and Health Posts in Brazil working as a medical lab technician, I wrote my mother almost one hundred letters which she saved for me for "my journal" as I asked her. Peace Corps paid us only about $600 a year to live on, the average income of people worldwide. I learned to live a very simple lifestyle which carried on with me for the rest of my life as did the memories of the happiness and hospitality of the poorer peoples of Brazil Most of the land and wealth in Brazil is held by a very few as in American now. We were taught in Peace Corps training that kind of disparity in wealth was the cause of the military dictatorship of Brazil in the 1960's.

During the last forty years, while thinking about my experiences in Peace Corps, rereading my letters, and writing this memoir, I have watched the environmental destruction of sweet, Mother Earth driven largely by the disparity between the poor and the wealthy. I have grown to despise the super rich, and now they control our government and the rest of the world. Mussolini called his form of totalitarianism, "Corporatism."

Peace Corps Syndrome

A mental and emotional condition created by; a preponderance of bureaucratic assholes; good intentioned meddling missionaries and governmental agencies; diseased, starving, dying children; man's own innate ability to overload his circuits (see "battle fatigue," *Webster's*); the greed of the 5% of the world's people who own and control 95% of the wealth, land, and use of resources…

Resulting in a condition whereby those afflicted with Peace Corps Syndrome feel guilt at luxury of any sort, often living lives with gaunt resources and amenities, are often advocates for the uneducated and poorer peoples of the earth, and who realize that Mother Earth cannot support man in the manner and style of the 5% who control her.

Ron Horton

We had seen the Amazon from thirty-five thousand feet sometime after midnight, and now at eight thirty in the morning we were suddenly diving almost straight down through solid clouds. As soon as we broke through the cloud cover of Rio's coastal mountains we were in full tropical sunlight only a few feet above the choppy ocean. The plane leveled off inches above white-capping waves and began an apparent suicide flight straight toward what I would later learn to be the famous Sugar Loaf Mountain. Just as I was about to extend my arm to fend off the tree limbs, the pilot dropped the left wing straight down, the right one straight up, and abruptly like a fighter pilot spinning in a 180 turn skipped right over the tops of the waves toward the ocean end of the landing strip.

As we approached the airport, I could see off to my left, feeding on a garbage dump, thousands of soaring black vultures. My god, this is how they feed them, I thought, on green Peace Corps Volunteers… plane crash victims. As we taxied up to the terminal and began to gather our carry

Peace Corps Syndrome

on luggage, the energy from our Amazon group, now reduced to about 30, was effervescent. I must have had 75 pounds of carry-on luggage as I walked out into the full tropical glare.

We were headed south down the coast, through Rio, heading for Praia Flamenco and the Hotel Florida, but to get there we had to grab a taxi from a long line of Volkswagens and Renaults with an occasional old 1950 Chevrolet thrown in. Our cab was a ridiculously small Renault with the right front seat removed. Dan _____, Rob _____, and I somehow fit about 15 bags on the floor in front and jumped in. For the first time in my life I had to speak Portuguese to someone who did not speak English. "Pria Flamenco, por favor...Hotel Florida."

Leaving the airport we drove past Rio's garbage dump where hundreds upon hundreds of the black vultures I had seen earlier made tornadic vortexes riding the coastal thermals in front of the jungle covered mountains that rose like mother earth's own giant green breasts.

Somehow, we actually arrived at the right place, at the Florida Hotel, and went in and registered. One of our medical group's chiropractors, Fred, and I wound up rooming together. We didn't expect to spend much time in Rio before we were to ship north to the Amazon, but that afternoon at our first indoctrination meeting the shit hit the fan. The national Peace Corps Director, a man I would soon learn to despise, looked up as one by one we entered his office to find out exactly which site would be ours. With utter disdain, he looked at me and said, "You're not going to the Amazon...we're shipping you to Mato Grosso; the director there needs another lab tech."

I had turned down going to the South Pacific to go to the Amazon, so I took his statement like a stab in my heart. After a moment of shock, I told him. "No damn way, I'm supposed to go to the Amazon".

"Well, you're going anyway." he said. When I threatened

to go home rather than oblige the stinking little bureaucrat, he said, "Okay." So within hours of arriving in country, I had been bureaucratically screwed. If I had realized just how much this would set the tone for the next two years, I probably would have gone back to the States.

Trained for the Amazon with the first full medical group in the Peace Corp, I was immediately shipped 1500 miles to the south; this bit of bureaucratic B.S. began to sink in as my training group flew off to the Amazon, and I flew south. South in South American means colder as north does in North America. Within a few hours of partying on Copacabana and Ipanema Beaches, clubs and sidewalk cafes, I landed in Cuiaba', the capital of Mato Grosso. At that time, this southwest frontier of Brazil was still a refuge for Nazi escapees. There were Brazilian soldiers everywhere, and I do mean everywhere since the military had overthrown the democratically elected government a few years before.

They put us up in a pensao, a hotel with a central courtyard and rooms on four sides. The walls only went up seven feet or so and all the rooms were open under one central, lofty roof. Sounds carried very well between rooms. A young lad could learn a lot about love making from surrounding sounds while trying to go to sleep in a strange place. We, Peace Corps Volunteers, ate out each night after long days of indoctrination and partied hard, so sleep came fairly easy if one was alone and night sounds were ignored... easy to do since we were usually smashed on rum.

How in the world had I gotten here, half a world away? In the summer of 1966, after graduating from Alabama College, a small liberal arts school in the central part of the state, I enrolled at Auburn University where a research assistantship had been finagled for me, making it possible to continue to work with Dr. Bob Mount, Alabama's

Peace Corps Syndrome

foremost herpetologist as he moved from Montevallo to Auburn. The year before, my senior year, my interest had turned from Art as I completed that major, and I began a study of snakes and turtles so intense that the hours spent searching paid off. I found a snake never before seen in Alabama. The black swamp snake, all of ten inches long, was found under some moss just inside Alabama, and was physically different in the number of scales of Florida samples. This was just enough for the world's smallest article in the first issue of the scientific journal ***Herpetologia***.

I had my entire herpetological career lined up. I would get my master's degree at Auburn with Mount and then go on to the University of Florida at Gainesville with Archie Carr, the world's foremost authority on sea turtles. At this time there was absolutely no danger of being drafted. Had I stayed in graduate school, the horror of what would transpire as I faced the draft two years later would be exacerbated by this fact.

President John Kennedy had started Peace Corps a few years before and had conned me with his, "Ask not what your country can do for you - ask what you can do for your country!" I had no chance against such a brazen plea. By 1966 the very first Peace Corps Volunteers were just returning home after service abroad and many major universities were awarding graduate school fellowships to them. My friend, Don, had joined Peace Corps the year before and was off in Ethiopia. Only weeks after I left for Brazil, he had to hide overnight in a pile of manure to keep from being shot by rebels who stormed his village. The chance to go adventuring in some far off land pulled me like a magnet.

Peace Corps first offered me Micronesia in the South Pacific: 10,000 islands, a training program consisting of sailing outrigger canoes, surf fishing, but somehow I accepted the chance to go with the first all medical group

Ron Horton

headed for the Amazon River. So, I withdrew from school, turned down my research assistantship, and unknowingly opened myself up to being drafted as soon as I got out of Peace Corps and the draft laws changed. But at the time, the draft was simply not a concern for me, so enmeshed was I in academia and the thrill of the adventure in Peace Corps.

A British history professor teaching Middle Eastern history in undergraduate school had intrigued me with tales of early English explorers seeking the source of the Nile, and when he said that no one had ever walked the length of the Nile, voila, there was my destiny...to walk the Nile. Hoorah for sophomoric exuberance! I would walk the Nile in complete ignorance of hundreds of miles of swamps, hundreds of miles of canyon lands, and thousands of crocodiles up to 25 feet, about the size of a Buick station wagon, sitting up on the banks waiting for little tidbits like me. Ignorance is bliss!

So off I went to Milwaukee of all places; Peace Corps training was brutal, 16-18 hours of classes in public health, tropical diseases, medical lab tech training, five hour language classes in the "Berlitz" style, i.e. endless repetition, plus a community development project. I volunteered to work with some inner-city Scout troops and with a Father Grokey, who later became quite well known for his efforts furthering civil rights, and I helped chaperone dances at his community center. I must have had the karma of an angel because we never had any trouble those nights that I worked with him. I enjoyed taking my black scout troop on hikes, but when I took them down to Lake Michigan to go swimming, the frigid water and floating human excrement upset me quite a bit, but the kids had a blast.

There was a big cafeteria on the ground floor of our Peace Corps housing, Hartman Hall, right on the main drag through town and the University of Marquette where we ate

Peace Corps Syndrome

and hung out between classes. People left training in droves; the attrition was quite high due to the intensity of the training and the reality of the health risks facing us. Thirty-five percent of all Peace Corp Volunteers, they told us, would catch amoebic dysentery.

1404 West Wisconsin Ave.
Hartman Hall
Milwaukee, Wisc.

Bon dia,

Things are hectic; we work all day long, you can't believe it. We start classes at 7:30 and go till 9:30-10:30 at night with a break for lunch and dinner. Five hours of language drill each day, comparative studies, a community development project to be initiated by ourselves, gym, health studies, etc.

They treat us damn well, good food. I just received tickets to two concerts. The dorm is co-ed. We have two MD's, one dentist, and ten nurses on our team.

They scare hell out of us, about de-selection, that is being dropped, and all the diseases we'll probably get. 35% get

Ron Horton

amoebic dysentery, 16 % amoebic hepatitis.
Send those Gulf bills to me. I left them in the living room, I believe. Send my watch if you can. I have your car keys. I'll mail them soon. If possible, send me some of those jeans (brushed denim) 31w.33L. Give my love. I must read now.
Ron

The pressure to excel on a personal level was constant, and I seemed to thrive on it, but the health risks involved were very real as they are today. (While sitting in a parasitology class twenty years later, in graduate school at the University of Arkansas, the girl sitting next to me, who had been a Peace Corps volunteer and was just back from Africa, had an enormous 12-inch long roundworm, Ascaris, crawl out of her nose.)

10 p.m. Tuesday

Hi,
It looks like I'm still a (lousy) letter writer with a typewriter. I received my box. The shirts are beautiful, that red nylon one is quite a conversation piece. If you remember, give me a list of all you sent, the box was terribly torn when it arrived. I got my billfold, watch, shorts, pants, watchbands, 3 shirts. If that's all don't bother about the list. The shirts are damned practical. I begin training Monday as a laboratory or medical technician. This I talked myself into, as it was set up for pharmacists, etc. It means a rougher schedule, if that is possible. I'll let you know more about it. I started the foundation tonight of a credit union among the trainees. We had a big speech last night about the establishment of such a community development (CD) project in Brazil, so I'm getting experience here. Had about 5 or 6 new faces Tuesday among my boys; carried them to Lake Michigan

Peace Corps Syndrome

for a swim. If anyone ever asks, it's filthy; the water's polluted with pure SHIT. You wouldn't believe it. It's swimming pools from now on.

We have mid-board selections next week. At this point you aren't de-selected if you are not good, but told what's wrong and given 5 weeks to correct it, which is a nice way of saying you get 5 more weeks, if they point out too many things. AT this point, I'm very optimistic about the whole thing. Training is almost half over. I hope I'll be speaking twice the Portuguese I speak now.

I'm really getting to know the people here now, and having a real blast. Some damn nice people, only one or two SOB's. We had a rain last night, and the filth on my screens was washed in on everything. You wouldn't believe how dirty it is here. Don't ever come here on vacation. The city smells of everything. It is terrible.

The medical technician training I mentioned will allow me to work in a health clinic in the mornings in Brazil and have the rest of the day for community development in agriculture, schools, etc. I have to study now. We got through at 9:30 and I have several hours before bed.

Ronnie

But the danger began even before we left the country. One of my roommates almost killed me by coming in drunk and catching his bed on fire; I'm alive simply because my head was right next to an open window. He was kicked out. Physical training was incessant, and I was very thankful that I had screwed up back at Alabama College when it came to finishing my Physical Ed requirements and had to take track and field my last semester in order to graduate. Though I smoked two packs of Camels a day, I was in great shape except when it came to endurance races. Peace Corps' physical training consisted of full field and track events; we were timed and pressured to do better as we were whipped into shape. On weekends we often played soccer, the first time for me, and I quickly volunteered to be goalie and not have to run 14 marathons like the rest of the players.

Summer of 1966

Dear Folks,
The Portuguese is coming along slowly. Just finished a 3 ½ hour lecture on some more of the health problems. Only had a 15 hour day.
My room mate won't make it though, I believe. He came in at 4:30, night before last, and must have dropped his cigarette (probably drunk). He woke up at 6:30 with his pillow and mattress on fire. I'm only a foot from a window and slept through it all. Then he threw his mattress in the bath tub; the pillow is totally ruined. He is attempting to hide it by switching the mattress from a vacant room, but the maid found the pillow and tomorrow the building inspectors come out for the purpose of finding out where the fire was, which won't be too hard since the wall above his bed is all smoked up.
We had three people leave already, more to go. These were all voluntary. The selective service should be checking on me by now. This is one of the most important things about making it. Say "Hi" to Ann and Clara and tell Bill Walker, "Hi."
I'm working with a negro Boy Scout Troop, carrying them camping, teaching them to swim and wrestle. I chaperoned about 200 negros at a dance at a Catholic Church with Fr. Grokey. It was the first night with no bottles, fights, or broken furniture. The idea is to simply get them off the streets, and it's working...they are developing manners,

etc. I must go. I have to study and its 20 minutes till midnight, and I wake up at 6:00 a.m.
Love,
Ron

5:15 p.m. Tuesday
Hi Folks:
I worked half the day in the Milwaukee County Hospital drawing blood. It's easy when you have a slim person with veins showing in his arms, but when you get an old fat person, you have to probe around. Sounds pretty ghoulish, doesn't it? Also, had my first day at the dentist; he cleaned them, and I mean cleaned them, and set up four appointments, with two more probable. He says that all four wisdom teeth are coming out. With what he did today and with all the stuff he gave me, he says that he can clear these bleeding gums of mine up. Another guy left last night; that makes seven now who have gone, and I can tell a few more are considering it. Tonight we have Portuguese until 10:30 to make up for a day last week when we had lectures. I have never been in better health; I weigh about 168-170. Wish Daddy Happy Birthday for me.
Only five and a half weeks to go and I will be home. You can't imagine how I'd love to be there. Ann dropped me a line last week. Oh, by the way, find more out about Don and let me know. If he is well enough, give him my address and ask him to write. I took some slides at the zoo here Saturday; if and when I get them developed, I'll send them home. That's about all for now.
Ate' amanha,
Ronnie

Often we were feted with a barbeque or a trip to one of Milwaukee's breweries on weekends. The camaraderie was unique and most of us became a tightly knit group of friends about to go off and save the world. I began to drink

Ron Horton

alongside my fellow Peace Corps Volunteers (PVC's) who drank every day. There was a nickel-a-glass beer joint right next door and the world's greatest chili joint four doors up, with about 50 kinds of chili, which of course required beer drinking.

It was 1966, and we were gung-ho Americans; our energy bubbled over several times a day with outbursts of folk songs. There were three guitar players in the group, and we'd sing the songs of the day, real sappy stuff, "Kumbaya," "Michael Row the Boat," and many others. Rob, whom I would later travel with for several months, was the best picker, and I often found myself hanging around the "babes" warbling along with him. Somehow I survived training, and if I could put time in a bottle, I would mark that period of time as "MAGIC" and visit it fairly often. So, a few months later, there I was, in the state of Mato Grosso, feeling a little bit put upon by the actions of Peace Corps bureaucrats. I had always played by the rules, but that didn't seem to be what mattered in Peace Corps.

Saturday, Oct. 8, 1966

Peace Corps Syndrome

Hi There,

I am sitting in a Pensao (Hotel) Lobby waiting to go to the airport in an hour. Have been here two days (under mosquito nets) in Campo Grande, the biggest town in the state of Matto Grosso. I am going to Cuiaba' tonight, and tomorrow to a town of 1000 called Alto Paraguay for two weeks to learn lab terminology in Portuguese and to learn to speak better. This hotel is rough. The lights go off all the time for extended periods...the first morning here we had no water, and so on, but I like it. Have met some nice people here, both volunteers and Brazilians. Yesterday, we went to a country club (in the country) and swam, played football (got blisters on my feet). The roads just a few blocks from the center of town are very rugged and most of the cars are Jeeps. The rainy season is about to begin here. It rained this morning. I went to a barbeque last night to the house of an American nurse who married a doctor here and met some of the most important people in the state. Several large landowners, cattlemen. One English couple named Horton, who have been here for 37 years. The father of the doctor is the largest land owner in the World, that's right! I'm beginning to think I don't want to work in a lab very much, but do other things, mainly. I'll have a chance to talk about this in two weeks when I return here and talk to the Boss man about a site. The Rep. and the Assistant Rep. are very nice people. In two weeks, I'll go to Dourango in the South. Alto Paraguay is in the North, for ten days or so. I'm about to go get a bite to eat. You have to be very careful what you eat and drink, very. The hotel clerk just took the book I was using to write on. Will mail this from Cuiaba' tonight. Will close now, just a sandwich (hot) and a beer. Can't drink the water without iodine.

Love,

Ron Horton

Ron
P.S. Please save my letters; they will be my journal. Give my love to all.

The pensao manager in Cuiaba' was a WW II Belgian refugee, a 50-year-old, large busted, red headed lady who must have had some unbelievable war stories to tell. She immediately adopted me and treated me like a long lost son. Out in the magnificent, tropical, central courtyard of the pensao, there were: breakfast melon trees (mamao), bananas, and some strange fruits I didn't recognize, one looked like a pear with a big pinto bean glued to the bottom that she named as cashew. She scolded me when I left the water running while I brushed my teeth and turned it off. "Turn it off until you need it," she grandmother barked. "Obrigado Senhora," I foamed toothpaste and answered. I was so green and so blatantly gung-ho, with this monstrous John F. Kennedy, "save the world grin," that most Grandmother Types immediately had their supportive systems on full alert. She later gave me a beautiful hand woven hammock and some jam when they shipped me to my site.

Oct. 11, 1966 12:30

Well, I'm sitting here in a broken bed among the flies in a town of 3000 called Alto Paraguay, which is north of Cuiaba' (get you a map). I went to the Health Post this morning, and have actually decided I don't want to work as a lab tech. I'm staying in a house that has the first toilet with a seat I've seen in 5 days. The big bugs don't bother you much, since the flies and mosquitoes fight too much to see who can attack you. I'll remain here until next Wednesday. It's a 6 hour bus ride over dirt roads back to Cuiaba'. Met a beautiful Peace Corp girl in Cuiaba', but she'll be sent to her site in the South this week. Every

Peace Corps Syndrome

night, except for last night, we've had a party or something. I went to an Elvis Presley movie (the only one showing in Cuiaba') night before last, and then to a party.

I'm living with a volunteer named Charles Johnson for these ten days. There's another volunteer in town, who is real silly and girlish and chubby. Carlos (Charles) is the athletic type and devoted to his work. We will get along well, I think. I'll be glad when these ten days are over, the seven day stay in the South, Dourados, and I can find out where my site is and go there.

By the way, mail gets through here and most packages to Mato Grosse, but number things anyway. I've given out of things to say, so I will close. Hope to go for a walk in the woods this afternoon. They have parrots, jaguars, etc. here and I want to see what they have. The other new PCV was sick and we left her in Cuiaba'. She'll be out today or tomorrow.

Your still well son,
Ron

    Before I got to my site, however, we had several weeks of indoctrination, and when I arrived in Campo Grande we were met by Rod and Bill, the junior administrators for Mato Grosso. Rod was a mid-western volunteer who had signed on for a second tour as an administrator. After arriving in Campo Grande, I was driven to my host family, a sweet group who happened to own the nicest restaurant in town. I roomed with their son, a pleasant 17-year-old, husky kid. All the other PCV's host families fed their American guests at their homes, but since my family left home early each morning to go to the restaurant, I would follow to lunch and sometimes supper at their place (12-15 tables on the outside, spread under gorgeous mango and

Ron Horton

palm trees, quite magical day or night). I loved their beef stroganoff which they made with cognac. But they always presented me with a bill or the waiter did, so while the other PCV's were eating free, I had to pay. After two weeks of this I had spent about a month's salary and never caught up financially for the next two years.

Dr. Bill ____ was my first educated black friend. I had black friends during college in Alabama in the mid 60's: musicians, university workers, etc., but most were still caught in the web of circumstance of being rural poor, with deep Southern accents and mannerisms. Not Bill! Bill was a 30-year-old New Yorker, only two years out of medical residency, a balding, stocky gentleman that everyone, man or woman immediately liked. With his smattering of eight or ten freckles on his light chocolate brown face, Bill exuded amiability, confidence, and cool. He was smooth, well dressed, neat, and a Karate aficionado, but one without menace.

Bill had arrived in country before I had hit town, and he set up shop as the physician for the Peace Corp Volunteers in the state of Mato Grosso, which is larger than the state of Texas. Coming from only a year and a half in private practice, replete with purple convertible and beautiful girlfriend, Bill had chosen the Peace Corp over Viet Nam. On arrival in Campo Grande, the southernmost large city in the state of Mato Grosso, Bill had been invited by the Brazilian military doctor, as a gesture of friendship and god knows what, to assist in what he thought to be a routine appendectomy at the military base. The military in Brazil in the 1960's were like the yuppies in the US in the 80's, everywhere, always in front of you, always acting like they knew whatever the hell they were doing had meaning. Anyhow, Bill went off to assist this doctor and everything was going along just fine, a regular appendectomy, when suddenly the patient began waking up... trying to sit up.

Peace Corps Syndrome

Since he was being cut wide open and having parts removed, he was a little agitated. At his first movement, Bill had looked at his Brazilian counterpart and said, "Hey, he's waking up; give him some anesthesia!" At this point, the Brazilian said, "Hey, that's all we have." Bill got to finish assisting by having to physically restrain the young soldier while surgery was completed. The patient recovered, but Bill never did.

This whole affair was only a harbinger of what his two years in Brazil would be like. Later, he would be off traveling and couldn't be found when my colleague, Janice, was having side effects from the rabies shots I was administering to her. Bill's second week in country saw his total downfall and the loss of his sane look at his host country. The first couple of experiences were, I think, directly responsible for Bill developing partying into a fine art.

As Bill told me a few weeks later, shortly after his arrival in country, he was downtown driving in his Willys Jeep at one of the main three or four intersections of Campo Grande when he saw a pedestrian trying to cross the street get knocked down by a car. The victim was in the middle of the intersection, but the car did not stop and neither did the other traffic. Bill sat and watched as cars from all directions kept going through the intersection, running over the victim repeatedly. He was finally able to help stop traffic and help until an ambulance arrived. Now, this is the same country that in the 1960's was taking the beggars off the streets in Rio de Janeiro and taking them off shore and sinking them, just as it did with tons of mail when the Post Office got backlogged too far.

These events in Bill's life affected him greatly. Having just gotten his medical practice set up, Bill had suddenly been given the option of Vietnam or Peace Corp, and in the course of a few weeks, was delivered from practicing medicine in New York and cruising in his lavender

Ron Horton

convertible to this scene in Camp Grande. Except for an occasional look at one of us 30 or 40 Mato Grosso, Peace Corps Volunteers, he had absolutely nothing but lots of time on his hands.

Bill had a typical Mato Grosso house five or six blocks from downtown: terra cotta roof, stucco walls, beautiful hardwood doors, tile floors, a backyard patio with broken jagged bottles on top of the walls, grape arbor, three bedrooms, hammocks out back, geckos on the ceiling, and a store on the corner that sold cheap liquor: Pinga, Cachacha, Brandy, and large, strong beer.

At that time, 10-cents American would buy a quart of 100-proof sugar cane Pinga, and that included deposit on the bottle. When I got to Brazil, I made about $45 American a month, or about 150,000 Brazilian dollars or cruzeiros. Cigarettes were 400 to 1000, matches 100, and they still had 1 and 5 cruzeiro bills...100 paper bills to buy a box of matches. Wads of paper money were in all pockets. I normally used currency for toilet paper in Brazilian bathrooms while traveling; it was better than the local T.P., when that was available.

Bill had a nineteen dollar, battery operated, Singer record player and five or six albums. The song, "Sonny Yesterday, to dah, duh,dah dah dah" was big then and was our main music at the many parties and dances we had at his house. Martinis were mixed in a three gallon soup pot, quart after quart of gin with less than 1/2 teaspoon of Vermouth, dry martinis dipped by the glassful. Bill would make a dramatic execution of adding one infinitesimal dollop of vermouth into the gin.

During most days in Campo Grande, we would drive downtown to the fried fish place, with its open doors on two sides and big deep pots of oil, cooking the best fish in the world. Pacus, two to four foot cousins of the Pirranah, Dorados and Pintados, six to eight foot green catfish with

Peace Corps Syndrome

large black spots, or any of the dozens of other delectable fish available for four or five hundred cruzeiros. We would munch on the tastiest, lightest, best fish I have ever eaten. Better than the Bream, Crappie, and on a higher level, better than fried Red Snapper or fresh baked King Mackerel steaks back home. We're talking fish. Then three or four caipirinhas, a strong drink, and it was "La-la Palooza" land. A caipirinha was three or four inches of 100-proof Pinga with lots of lime and two tablespoons of sugar: one and you were slightly numb; three and you were drooling.

If we were at lunch, two of these drinks seemed to stir us enough to handle most afternoon adventures, usually at the country club. The Campo Grande Country Club had invited Bill into their fold and consisted of a fenced, adequate swimming pool, dressing rooms, and refreshment counter. But the real luxury was the parties held when Bill's two other New York friends would come in from their posts in the North, and we would come from the South. Both friends had that sarcastic, hard, New York lip that brought out the best in Doc Bill.

These sojourns into Campo Grande to see Bill were the only reprieves from the real insanity of living in our remote villages where we lived with people who made less that $600/year... 95% of the population, by the way, and where luxuries were unknown. Coming into town often meant a full day on a Mercedes bus or several buses and trains. Parties got pretty wild as the tropical nights progressed. Often the ladies would wind up wearing only tee-shirts. One such party, a send-off for a departing Peace Corps Volunteer, written up in our state Peace Crops news-letter, described the dress as "White Tie and Tails."

One afternoon there were about eight of us at Bill's house, sitting as we rarely did in his living room; usually we gravitated to his gorgeous back yard and patio under the typical grape arbor, festooned with hammocks. Bill had a

Ron Horton

very impressive, neatly stacked pile of at least 50 cachaca and brandy bottles lined up under the plastered, eight foot wall with its dozens of broken, jagged, glass shards sticking up out of the mortar atop, the usual Brazilian wall adornments. I had only just arrived from Dourados for the rest of my rabies shots (the details of this ordeal will come later). Bill was showing me his collection of switchblades, those weapons that were outlawed in the US; he had just picked up the newest one in Bolivia while flying back to Campo Grande from Cuiaba'. As we sat in his living room, Pam, Vivian, the Scarsdale loudmouth, Janice and a couple of others, Bill began talking about hypnotism and soon dared us to be attentive and that he would mesmerize the lot of us. So we all took deep breaths and closed our eyes as he bade us. It was quite hypnotic as he smooth talked us into something akin to meditation, which I had not included in my life at the time. Perhaps it was the cachaca or just me, but I somehow failed to go under.

One of the volunteers, Gladys, was a forty-year-old lab tech who had been taking male hormones and had a mustache; she told me this story in an age when homosexuality and such just wasn't talked about. One topic was mentioned, however, and got gasps from most of us when I asked Bill, "What was your most unusual case?" He grinned and told us a tale about working an emergency room shift where a guy came in with a Vaseline jar up his butt. Bill said the guy told a story about being with a group of friends all bragging about the largest things they could get up their alternate love canals, the patient had somehow gotten the medium, "not the small jar" Bill added with emphasis. "We had to use delivery forceps on the idiot."

One night after a party at Bill's we decided to go to the club for a moonlight swim. There must have been about 12-15 of us crammed into his Willys as we tore through town, at least five people crammed into the front seat...Gladys sitting shotgun. We were all real drunk and

Peace Corps Syndrome

as Bill did a very exaggerated turn to the left, Gladys' door flew open and she flew out, grabbing the top of the rolled down window. I was the only one apparently aware of her outside the car, legs bouncing all over the road, getting scraped. I looked at her and over the heads of the others in the front seat, to Bill at the wheel, and back to Gladys and thought, I'd better say something. Finally, I hollered for Bill to stop. We had to take Gladys back to her place where she assured us that she could doctor herself before we went on our skinny dipping swim at the club. The night watchman actually showed up about two in the morning and told us we needed to leave.

On those rare occasions when several of us made it out to the club with Bill in the daytime we had to wear bathing suits, which almost appeared to be optional when I looked at the younger, string bikini set. Bill would inevitably begin the slowest, back-stroke laps ever demonstrated upon this earth, his light tan, freckled, watermelon stocky stomach outshining his bald head while his swimming movements could not be ascertained by the naked eye. It seemed each stroke took five minutes for the arm to saunter alongside his head; once I thought a ripple actually moved off the chocolate iceberg seemingly adrift. But a little later I'd notice he was in another part of the pool still pretending that he was doing laps.

Often when we got this drunk, which was every gathering, Bill would demonstrate his Karate expertise. I was testeroned enough to be his foil and would await his full blown charges, with Bill four feet off the ground, arms cocked back to karate chop me, which he usually did.

Bill had a lady friend come visit from the States, and we were all happy for him, but I think his true love was another sweet thing back home.

Ron Horton

ATTITUDE TOWARD ANIMALS AND THE ENVIRONMENT

I'm going to have to stick in several little notes to explain things as we go along; this one seemed the most important in retrospect. I am so ashamed of my attitude toward animals and the ecosystem back in the 1960's. These days I'm a staunch environmentalist, once having spent 103 days in a 300-year-old, giant, Live Oak tree to save it from being cut. However, in the mid 1960's one didn't think much about taking from the environment as when I bought jaguar, anaconda, and giant anteater skins. I find this so repulsive now that I can't recognize myself forty years ago.

Oct. 14, 11:00 am

Hi,
I caught a boa constrictor yesterday, 4 feet long. Also have a tarantula as a pet. It's been an exciting few days. Have seen a lot of wildlife; I went diamond mining as I think I told you. And have seen handfuls of stones from the rich landowners. Am now in Cuiaba' destined for Sao Antonio (where I went on a picnic last weekend) for three or four days for my partner in Alto Paraguay has a kidney infection and is here to see the witch doctor. Sao Antonio is nice, a fishing town on a river. I hope to talk to the fishermen to great ends as I would like to work with them possibly in other towns. Am back in town with the female PCV I mentioned. She is sharp, but nothing is sparking, I think, so I guess I will find me a native wench.

Since I will have little time to write all, why don't you tell Ann, Bill, and Clara what's up at times for me. Really hate

Peace Corps Syndrome

to crash in on his guy in Sao Antonio, but it's not my choice. Will be awfully glad to get back to Campo Grande next Saturday or Friday with the others; am getting sore pressed to get to work. Will close to get these to the Post Office before lunch.

Your well and hungry son,
Ron

Santo Antonio Oct. 19, 9:30 am

Hi There,
Well, we're now the proud owners of a monkey, aged two months. I don't know the type. I thought she was dying this morning; she was strangled on milk. It's raining very heavily here at the Health Post and no patients have showed up. I'm back in Santo Antonio until tomorrow morning and then to Cuiaba'; it's an hour away by bus, and then by plane to Camp Grande, about 600 miles to the South. I visited an old woman potter and weaver in the country yesterday. Her daughter was there with 4 children, all boys; I gave the boys a chocolate bar and it was the first any of them had ever had, including the mother. They lived in a mud and stick house, dirt floor, and it was the cleanest house I've ever seen. The floor and yard were spotless, well swept.

I'm starving right now; the breakfasts are nothing, coffee and bread; I've told you this but thought I would mention it again. I received your first letter yesterday. Have received no others. Had a slight case of diarrhea yesterday, but it has stopped. Toilet paper here is newspaper or magazines. At times you shower by the bucket system. Just saw a pig running for shelter, so I will close now.
Still well,
Ron

Ron Horton

Oct. 31, 9:30 am

Ma, Pa, and Rhonda,

You wouldn't believe the mud here. Went to Paraguay (country of); bought some Pall Malls. Saw a possible site Saturday, southeast of Dourados, called Vila Brasila, nice spot. As a test to see if boots will get through (I don't remember about my grey suede boots, if I packed them or not) if you will, and they aren't too much, mail the grey suede, airmail to Campo Grande, keep them dirty in case some greedy mail clerk decides he wants some boots, this might change his mind. We're not doing a damn thing yet. Am spending too much on Hotel, etc., but for training we are given more so it will work out fine. Oh, today is Halloween, we just explained Halloween to 6 Brazilian men. Will close.

Ron

FLYING on DC-3's and C47's

It was pretty exciting flying in the state of Mato Grosso,

Peace Corps Syndrome

since it was always on World War II vintage, twin engine veterans. Flying from Cuiaba' to Campo Grande the first time out, we flew west toward the Bolivian border before turning back south. The landing strip was on a round hill side, so as we landed with one wing a lot lower than on the uphill side, we quickly went around the small clearing on the hill, out of sight of where we had first hit the ground amidst solid thick jungle. Flying back the other way into Cuiaba' later that year I got to watch a big bolt vibrate loose from the engine mount as dark approached, and some nearby passengers began to lament the fact that Cuiaba's airport had no lights for night time landing. I didn't start to worry much until I looked out into the pitch blackness. From where I was sitting, I could see into the back of the engine where a really big part of it was red hot and glowing in the dark. As we made our approach, I actually appreciated the glowing engine part as we landed since it was the only thing that stood out in the darkness as we bounced down. Later while I was in Dourados a small plane came into the unlit airport, and since he couldn't land, began to buzz the main street over and over until a bunch of cars and trucks tore off to line both sides of the runway and saved the passengers. I'm amazed our pilot didn't do the same over Cuiaba'.

The flights to and from Rio or Sao Paulo were on beautiful, 4 engine, Rolls-Royce Viscounts. I still remember the beautiful purr of those engines that I saw so many times, occasionally going to Rio or Sao Paulo for mid-service conference, but a lot more often when we were seeing other PCV's off to the States. I've often thought those trips out were probably rewards for them forgetting to pay us twice for four months. I'm serious; the sons of bitches left us green kids out in the jungle, without money, which meant no food or shelter, unless we somehow could display magical powers thousands of miles from home. I was so far south I was bitterly cold for months each year, no heat, no hot water, no warm clothes, houses with open eaves, could barely speak the language, and the people thought I was CIA; that's the real Peace Corps.

Cuiaba', Nov. 7, 12:45 pm

Hi,
I'll be getting my site today or in the morning. The Brazilian Boss indicated he wants me in the South, Vila Brasil, but I have a chance for San Antonio, where I was, which has a male volunteer, but it appears he's about to be drafted. He's served two years and this is his third.

Am well again,
Ron

Nov. 10, 9:00 am

Folks and Rhonda,
I'm on a DC-6 (one of the old two-engined jobs), flying toward the Brazilian-Bolivian border to a city called Curumba. On from there to Dourados, by way of Campo Grande by bus and plane, and somehow 40 kilometers on to Fatima do Sul. It all seems unreal, here, flying over this Pantanelle, which is a swamp like massive area, that when cleared, is one of the best places for cattle in the world.

It should be damned exciting these first few days in Fatima do Sol. I don't know if I told you, but I'll probably have a horse, compliments of the Peace Corps. Saw what I wanted for Christmas yesterday; forget everything else. A guitar, which one of the volunteers bought; you can get a beautiful guitar for 70 or 80 thousand, that's about 35 dollars. (Our P.C. training team had consistently told us how to pick up

Peace Corps Syndrome

extra money i.e. buy whiskey at New York and sell in country, take Kennedy half dollar coins, a hot item to Catholic Brazilians who all had a photo of him on their walls.)

I'm going to get me a house this first week...need to go slow though and get one at a good price. Hoping to get one for 25 mil (thousand) a month and food for 45 to 60 mil. The hotel owner Cuiaba', an old lady, fell in love with me as a son, helped me sell my whiskey I got in New York and Paraguay, gave me a hammock, and a jar of marmalade, and hugged me on my way this morning. The hede (hammock) is two years old, in good shape; I'm going to dye it bright blue, it cost 70 mil new. I paid for my hotel bill and made 28 mil selling the whiskey to Her-sed, another friend. So in essence, I wound up buying the two boots for about 25 mil. I'm turning into a trader. The boots will go for 100 mil or more, easily. The situation is looking better. Also got my settling in allowance...150 mil... for moving essentials. Will be awfully glad when these first days are over and I get used to my site. Will close. Ron

Ron Horton

Nov. 13, 10:00 am

Dear Mom,
There is an American-Brazilian priest returning to Mato Grosso from Boston in January. I have met a friend of his, and have been given the o.k. to send the priest a few things for him to bring down to me. It's cold here in the South and should be getting warmer as we're in the middle of spring down here. I was thinking of asking you to ransack a little for me and mail them to Boston. These are a few of the things I thought of, trying to keep it small and light, and the things I need the most: my tan and green sweater, a pair of tennis shoes, 4 or 5 packages of plastic bags, and 3 or 4 pairs of socks.

I'm hoping to find a house soon in Fatima do Sul (new name for Vila Brazil). I now have a bicycle, and a cot with a bed frame and a chair coming. It was very chilly last night here. I slept under a blanket and a spread, but these and their beds are about 4 ft. long, it seems, and my toes stick out. It is warm now and slightly cloudy, very muddy, and a quiet Sunday afternoon. We had an eclipse yesterday, but I couldn't see it. Say "Hi" to all. Haven't gotten a letter in about a week; it's the constant change in address.

Love,
Ron

Nov. 15, 4:30 pm

Hi Folks,
I arrived in town, priced one place for room and board, 100 mil, the second place, 70 mil, when I re-met a guy who works for the State Agricultural Board. He's living in an unused technical school, 6 apartments, two large

Peace Corps Syndrome

classrooms, a kitchen, individual baths, and he asked me to live here. My new boss lived here until May of this year. My room is about 30 by 15 feet, 18 feet of closet, inlaid wood floors, sliding windows, gray wood work, light bluish gray walls. I'm doing my other stuff in bright orange and blue to contrast. I made some bookshelves with two boards and some blocks, sleeping on a cot, have a large table and two chairs. No electricity! Possibly soon. My gas container on the stove is empty, will get some tomorrow; today is election day. I'm on the border of town, thick green fields for 150 feet, then trees on one side, fields on another. I can get a big dinner for 30 mil a month, plan to cook my own breakfast and supper. We'll see. Bought a sheet, bed spread, 2 towels, glasses, plates, etc. yesterday. There were already some brooms, some pans, a meat grinder, etc. here. The shower is very cold. My windows on one side are 10 by 6 and about 12 by 6 on the other. It's going to take a lot of material to cover them. Barbosa da Costa, the guy living here is gone this week. It was lonely last night; I read. Going to the show tonight. Everything is closed, and I can't buy gas and other things for the kitchen. I haven't talked to my Brazilian boss yet. He's in Dourados; I'm going on Thursday or Friday to see him and go to a Thanksgiving-farewell party at a Fazenda around Maracaju, which is north of here. I'm about to go see how the elections came out and rest.

There's been a survey (Health) done in 1963-64, so my first few weeks will be to check this out and then update it. I'm going in Monday. The girl here is about 23 or 24, plain and a hard worker. I don't know if I mentioned it or not that a nurse I traveled with in Milwaukee might come down, it all depends how she likes the temporary site. She wants to teach nursing and practice too, we'll see. I just scrubbed the floor and got half the window covered. Am starving. Send me some simple recipes.

Ron Horton

Love,
Ron

Nov. 20   7:00 pm

Hi,
I've received one letter, no two, and Ann's about two weeks ago, nothing since. Hope it's waiting when I get back home. I'm at Al B_____'s fazenda, about 4 hours north of me. We had about 25 people or more for the party I wrote you about. Met three Swiss people, one spoke English and Swiss, the other two Portuguese and Swiss. Al's mother spoke Spanish and English, and there I sat with myself. I spent 6 hours in the saddle Saturday driving cattle across 33 square kilometers of beauty. Today we had turkey, cranberry sauce, stuffing, gravy; of course I had the turkey leg. I'm stuck here and have to take three buses tomorrow to get back. It will be 4 or 5 tomorrow before I get home. I don't relish this. At last, I'm going to begin work. Met my chief and he seems to have given me full reign.

I'm back home. My house was robbed of all my food and dishes, about 40-50 mil. Had my first day at work. The thieves did leave my potatoes, a cucumber, and a coffee pot. Haven't gotten a card from you in I don't know how long.
Ron

What a hell of a three days.
How are All? Give my love around

Saturday, Nov. 26   8:00 pm

Hi,

Peace Corps Syndrome

I got a letter from you, mailed on the 15th of November, on the 24th, saying you had received a letter which said I had received your first letter. Does that make sense? I'm averaging 2 to 3 a week to you. Perhaps you can go roughly by dates on mine rather than numbers, since I'm so damned bad about numbering. Am going ape waiting for my trunk. My finger is not broken, it's been a week and is still very swollen, but the x-ray says no break. Also got some money from Janice here. What with my thief and doctors bills, I was getting short.

Did you get my letter about the priest? If not, please respond immediately. He's in the States and coming down in January. If you have the letter add 2-$1.00 cartridge fountain pens and some light, small, cheap things like small super balls for presents, birthday for kids and girls. Possibly a package or so of razor blades for presents too.

We just finished dinner here. It's night and very dark. I'm going back early in the morning; it's 1 ½ hours by bus to have lunch with a guy I met in my town. Have to get a map of the city for my work. Going to meet the Padre also this week. I'm having the frames for my screens made also. The work will be good as soon as I broaden it. Going to pass out some garden seeds to my neighbors. Got them today.

Love,
Ron

JANICE

The first time I met Janice, who was stationed down south in Dourados, I was in a jeep with Tom J_____, a new temporary state director. The state director who had separated me from my friends and the Amazon had returned to the States. My kidnapping now appeared even more childish and inane. This new temporary director was a regular fellow, a field volunteer like me, who had been asked to fill in until a new state director could be trained. "You'll love Janice," Tom said, as we drove through billowing clouds of red dust. "She'll put you up at her place whenever you're in town," he said, as we drove into the town of Dourados. I was to be stationed three hours to the south; Janice was on the bus route that I would frequent when traveling north to the state capital for our regular conferences and parties.

Janice was a voluptuous, thirty-five-year-old, blond headed, freckled faced nurse. She was gorgeous, but she did have a few personal problems. She was a virgin when I met her; every patient that she had seen as a leukemia ward nurse for fifteen years had died; she had a reversed gender Oedipus complex with a domineering father; she was Catholic; and she drank like a fish. However, she was not really atypical of many of the older Peace Corps Volunteers; she had jumped at the chance for a major life style change when John Kennedy offered her an altruistic way to radically change her dead-end life and fled a Boston children's hospital, unable to handle losing another child that she would inevitably grow to love with her spacious heart.

Janice was perpetually effervescent and her blue eyes sparkled when she met us at her doorway. I noticed that she was surrounded by eight to ten kids, seven to twelve-year-old boys and girls in shabby shorts, the older girls the only ones wearing cotton blouses. The little rascals stood barefooted in the dust of the courtyard driveway, three or four brown kids hanging on to her as she talked, holding her hands or wrapped around her freckled legs. She was from Boston and had that classic John Kennedy way of speaking where Cuba became "Cuber." The year-and-a-

Peace Corps Syndrome

half or so that I would spend with her changed my way of speaking so much that when I returned from Brazil in 1968 and called Mom from New York, I thought she was putting me on, her southern accent seemed so accentuated. I actually laughed at her until she got angry, and I had to apologize. Janice would change the way I speak to the point where, until this day, people never believe that I'm from Alabama.

"Hey, Janice," Tom said, as we jumped out of the Willys Jeep.

Janice's front door was wide open; there was no way to keep the critters out, anyway, I soon learned,

"This is Ron Horton."

She grabbed my hand and grinned through a million freckles, her light, yellow-blond hair resting on her bare shoulders, the speckled and tanned tops of her ample breasts showing above her cotton blouse, loosely held up by half inch wide straps. I was twenty-three years old, six feet two, one-hundred-sixty-five pounds, a kid in the truest, naïve sense, and she was a woman in her prime. She was voluptuous in a "Doris Day" way. Aware of her womanhood's affect on men other than her father for apparently the first time in her life, she was like a perfectly ripe peach needing to be bitten into before the ripeness changed to sour. She and I became best friends over the next 18 months, and I got to see her blossom as she fell in love with an Argentine-English rancher and loved what I'm sure was the only man in her life.

Her brick apartment was one of 30 or so on the outskirts of town near the jungle. The apartments were built in six to eight unit complexes, about 30 feet across from each other. It was a lot cooler in the red tile floored building than in the tropical sun as Tom and I entered the shade, stepping out of the white hot, two o'clock tropical sauna. The main room was a combination living room with a kitchen in the back; bedrooms were off to the left. Out the back door across a tile floored, walled terrace was a brick shower and bathroom, and a little enclosed back yard.

"You guys want a beer?" "Sure," we both panted. "Aeulide, vem ca," she said to an 11-year-old, light brown haired boy. "Go get us three beers," handing him a wad of orange and yellow money. "You can have the change." He scooted out the front door on a dead run, two other boys tagging along. He was back with three big lukewarm beers in about three minutes, having run to a bar on the corner that had a cooler. As I sat down and popped my beer, there was suddenly an eight-year-old girl leaning on my left shoulder and three of the boys were leaning on my knees, within a foot-and-a-half to two feet from my face, the "fishbowl effect" we had been trained to expect from third world kids constantly watching us strange Americans.

For the next two years I would almost always be surrounded by a flock of good natured, smiling faces, always ready for an adventure, a laugh, or an errand. They were usually at Janice's apartment; she would constantly make little snacks for them to try or would have some project going on with the kids involved. Sadly, every day on the way to work or while traveling one would see several dying children, the swollen stomachs of Kwashikora, a severe protein deficiency, grotesquely deforming their emaciated bodies. Many of the children had only bread to eat, maybe some black beans or rice too, but rarely enough. Forty years later, I can still see the smiling faces of Janice's kids as clearly in my mind as at that first moment.

Americans were rare there on the frontier, but American movies were shown in the local movie house, and the Brazilians loved us gringos. They would almost come to blows with each other in attempts to entertain us, house us, and befriend us in spite of the fact that almost all believed we were C.I.A. agents. I'm serious; the Brazilian

Peace Corps Syndrome

national press, or at the very least their trash magazines, were constantly full of what I then thought to be crap.

The stucco walls of Janice's apartment were painted a shade of brown close to the color of the dust swirling down between the complexes. I had arrived in the middle of the dry season; it would be another three months before the six month rainy season began; a classic Mediterranean climate pattern. On the drive into Dourados, I had noticed fires and smoke from several ranches and farms. Such large areas were being burned to clear jungle for grazing or subsistence farming that the smoke, combined with the dust, created a smog that covered large sections of the continent for months at a time. You couldn't see more than half a mile.

Janice set me up in her spare bedroom, and after Tom left I took a shower. Wearing nothing but blue jeans, I was unpacking my clothes when I heard a horrible, large noise outside. It was almost last light as I ran out the back door. Right above my head, about 40 feet up, were thousands and thousands of green parrots screaming and squawking and flying with a great flapping of wings. What a welcome! I watched in amazement for several minutes, just as night fell, before I walked back into the apartment and hit the light switch. Nothing happened. Just then I heard a diesel engine crank about 100 feet away. Janice was outside doing something with the kids when I noticed the filament in her kitchen light beginning to glow, but it never got bright. The electric generator was so weak that it hardly ever made the light bulbs incandesce or whatever they do to really put out light. You could stand six-inches from the light bulb and stare directly at the filament, turn and walk into the dark and not have your vision impaired while your eyes adjusted from light to dark.

Janice had a pork roast cooking in a big aluminum pot on a small, white enamel, conventional gas stove. There was a small propane tank on the floor beside it. We laughed about the lights while she said that we only had electricity for three hours each night. That explained the Aladdin kerosene lantern on the kitchen table.

"Want a drink," she said.

"Sure," I responded, and she handed me a glass jelly jar two-fifths full of rum and then set down a coke beside my glass. Cuba Libras! She would hand me hundreds of such drinks over the next 18 months, and I would hand her hundreds.

Every Peace Corps experience revolved around drinking, and Janice was no exception; on the contrary, she was an expert. Janice taught me to drink. We would have five or six drinks almost every night. We often drank gin and tonic, the quinine helping to protect us from malaria. This first evening together we sat around her kitchen table.

After checking the pork roast, she plopped down across from me, freckles dripping off her arms and legs, and proceeded to tell me her life story. Everything that is, except for the Oepidus thing with her father, which I figured out in short order. This was not that amazing an accomplishment for a naïve 23-year-old to ascertain; the crush she had on her dad was that blatantly obvious. We usually got pretty shit faced in the evenings as we visited, listening to the BBC on her short-wave.

Keeping the station in tune required almost constant fine tuning. The BBC was our only link with the outside world; they told us about the war in Viet Nam almost every day, the Chicago Democratic National Convention riots, the assassinations of Dr. Martin Luther King and Robert Kennedy. At nine o'clock the electric generator shut down with a long whine. On my next trip out across the patio to whiz, I was astounded at the millions and millions of stars; on the way back inside I stopped for a moment and Janice came out and stood beside me. The kids were all gone by this time of the night. We bathed in star-glow for several minutes; Janice looked back to her right and pointed at stars I had never seen before, a big constellation she called the

Peace Corps Syndrome

Southern Cross.

After a few months stationed three hours south, I moved and rented an apartment a few doors down from Janice, and for about a year and a half, we worked in the same Health Post in Dourados. I was a medical laboratory technician and Janice was a nurse. I mainly did stool exams for worms and blood samples for malaria and tuberculosis. Our positions in the Health Posts were redundant, although, there were moments at the first when I was in charge of the lab that I felt we were doing some good. For the most part we were not really needed there.

RABIES

I had several dogs with rabies when I was growing up in Alabama since I was constantly rescuing strays. When I was about ten a stray dog got hit by a car a block from the house, and when I tried to get it out of the road, he bit me. Dad had to cut its head off after it died to have it checked for rabies. Another mutt I brought home literally went mad directly under my bed, outside under the house, and had to be picked up by the dogcatcher.

I made several good Brazilian friends and young Noe E_____, one of the first, a budding naturalist, and his German immigrant family quickly adopted me when I finally settled into my first site at Fatima Do Sul. I had a great photo of me in the jungle swinging on a vine during one of our visits. "Brachiating" is the verb, and I always listed it for one of my hobbies. Soon Noe and I had a truly unbelievable collection of dozens of iridescent beetles and hundreds of butterflies.

Once, just when I got ready to travel by bus from Fatima to Campo Grande, Noe came over to my place and told me about an exotic little rodent he had just captured, an ajouti or something. Actually, he wanted me to help him transfer it from his trap to a cage, but when he opened the trap, something slipped and BAM, I was bitten quite badly. As he wrapped up my finger, I said, "Whatever you do, don't let it escape; we'll have to quarantine it for two weeks to check for rabies." A week later, when I returned from Campo Grande, Noe had a sheepish grin on his face when I showed up at his house. "It got away Ronaldo." "Oh no," I moaned as I turned around and went straight back to the bus I had just ridden on for six hours to go back to Dourados. Janice soon set up giving me the rabies series which she got from one of the Health Post doctors, but we didn't have refrigeration and couldn't store the vaccine, so I had to go into Campo Grande and stay with Dr. Bill for the rest of the 14 day duration of the shots. Strangely, a year later I would be giving Janice the rabies series in her tightly freckled belly.

Bill started me on the shots, which had to be given in the abdomen; back than I had really tight abs (I was 6' 2," 165 pounds, a 31 waist, 33 inch inseam…a real string bean. Though ten pounds lighter going into the 11th grade, I had played first string DEFENSIVE TACKLE for one of the better football teams in Alabama), and the injections hurt like hell, no matter what I told my mom in letters back home. Bill and I both would usually be tanked up pretty good on two or three caipiringas before looking for spots where he hadn't shot me before. Janice had given me the first few. She was very efficient giving shots, though I usually got distracted when she loosened up my britches a little, just like I was one of her pre-teen leukemia kids back in Boston.

A year later several animals in the neighborhood began to act crazy and suddenly died. As Janice and I tried to figure out what was happening, all five of her cats died in the same manner. She somehow deduced they had died from a rarer form of rabies; insipid rabies is what it's called. Unfortunately, she had been bitten several times when tending her pets during their last days. One by one she had tamed the starving wild beasts, first the mother cat and her kittens; we were amazed at the way the mother would save some of her food for an enormous black tom that at first would only come in late at night. He became one of our favorites, and their deaths really saddened the two of us.

I had turtles, snakes, monkeys, a parrot, caged and free rabbits, ducks and several other critters at my place. My big, pet, house rabbit died in the same mysterious way. We tried to contact Dr. Bill, but he was off somewhere and couldn't be found. Somehow Janice found refrigeration for the vaccine. So I began to inject her freckled, tight tummy, just as she had injected me the year before. It was very emotional for both of us.

After six or seven of the shots, Janice began to develop several of the dangerous side effects listed on the vaccine label. I forget all she complained about, but I do remember stiffness of the spine really bothered her. Remember now, Janice was a 15 year, veteran nurse, wise in her field, but when we still couldn't find the Peace Corps doctor, we were scared shitless to put it bluntly. What to do? Stop the series and maybe get rabies or continue and paralyze her or something worse. Finally, about day eight or so Bill drove up in front of her door and quite easily said, "That's enough shots."

The Peace Corps office in Rio had been bombed a few weeks before; no Americans were injured, but a Brazilian national had his hand blown off. Some fantastic prosthesis, at the time, that connected to nerves or something was available for American government workers but not for nationals. Bill doctored some papers and pretending the guy was a PCV had flown with him back to the States and gotten the prosthesis operation for the Brazilian. He had just returned to Brazil and came straight to us.

Ron Horton

Dec. 2   8:30 a.m.

Hi There,

I'm in Dourados on my way to Campo Grande for my rabies shots at Janice's house. I would have been about halfway there but the bus driver forgot to tell me to get off at another stop, so I'm having to wait 6 hours, and will arrive tonight. Haven't heard from you yet about the priest. Do you have the address and all? Throw in a map of Alabama and one or two rolls of film; it's only 66 cents at Miller's. I don't think all this will get into much money, don't let it. Oh, guess what! Terzinha. my co-worker is taking a months vacation, and I'll be running the Health Post by myself.

If you see Don, tell him I'm well and healthy and would like to hear from him. If you see any good gossip columns in the Bessemer News send it. I'm going to send a roll of film home, some of New York and Home. I don't remember entirely (black and white). I'm going to try to get some packages to Rhonda, Johnny, and David. Tell Bill I said hi. Pass my news to him and tell him I'll write him. Do you have his address?

If it snows, put some in an envelope and send it down, they haven't seen it here. I can just see the leafless trees and the gray skies and rain and Lakewood at Christmas and all the hustle and bustle of the season.
My finger is still grossly enlarged, glad the Doctor is going to have a chance to look at it.

Met some good people this week; the cutest are four little girls, dirt poor, who live behind my house. They are full of smiles and giggles and call me Senhor (Sir). Hope to give

Peace Corps Syndrome

them a Christmas. Still no pets at my house except for two gopher toads. My apartment still doesn't have my touch yet. Still a little lifeless and cold.

Six hours on the bus. uhh-! That's going to be as much fun as the shots. Will close, it's about 9:05 and I'm going to straighten out my finances, eat, and catch the bus.

Your unlucky son,
Ronald Horton
P.S. Merry Christmas all and Happy New Year.

7:15 December 5

Hi,
Looks as if I will have a PCV nurse stationed with me. Hurray! Got your letter with the dollar and the other with 7 cents due marked on it, but who has change for a dime in Brazil. Thanks a lot...enjoyed the cartoon. A dollar will soon be 3/5 of a day's wages here when inflation sends the dollar to 3000 cruzeiros, and it goes a long way beyond the 5000 per day I'm getting. The rabies injections aren't really very bad. Going back to Campo Grande tomorrow after two days here. Had to find refrigeration for the vaccine as it only lasts three days without it. Going to take about 7 days around Christmas so I can be there till New Years. No other excitement. I may have to give them (the shots) myself after Thursday. Umph! Bye. Merry Christmas.

Your well son,
Ron

Ron Horton

Campo Grande Dec. 13, 10:45 a.m.

Hi,

Just found a letter I wrote the 2nd and forgot to mail, will send it along also. Have now had 12 of my 14 shots. Going back down Friday, with Vivian, I hope. Will stay till the 24th and come back up for Christmas with the whole Mato Grosso group. I haven't really begun to do a damn thing. Will be relieved to work for a week. Still no word on my trunk.

Doing little here. I am working on the Health Survey map I mentioned. It's a lot of painstaking drawing with ruler. Helped Doc Bill clean his yard yesterday. Am getting 8 mil extra per day here and it's taking it. My check for Jan. and Feb. is waiting at home with the 10 mil raise which comes to 330 mil. Right in the bank it goes. Hope this gets there before Christmas. I feel embarrassed to introduce Vivian to my Brazilian chief. Down there for 5 weeks, I've been on the job for 3. Oh hell, huh. Our Post is going to be a

41

Peace Corps Syndrome

swinger soon, with doctor, nurse, lab tech, etc. I'm going to cut my mosquito net up, clean the birds out and nail the net up to keep them out. About to walk down to the office and grab lunch. Merry Christmas again. Have a good one.
Am off to the office.
Ron

Date Unknown

Folks,
My average lunch is a large amount of beans and rice, a small filet, hamburger cooked in a tomato sauce, green beans, potatoes, cucumbers, tomatoes, bread dessert, coffee, very good attention by 13 year old waitress; this is for 1mil/day or 30 a month.
Meeting several friends of Ken C____'s, who is coming this week to be the temporary new boss; I may have mentioned this. Getting to be a friendly place. The cinema looks like a Montana Dance Hall of the 1880's, the floor slopes down and then up, the screen is nailed on, floor is brick, construction is unpainted wood, all very rustic; one of the advertisements is for "Captain Jungle." Serial #2, looks like the Phantom in comics, must be a real old one. Bought a container of gas and a hammer, having trouble finding the right size material for drapes, one window in 9 ft. by 4 ½, the other is about 12 ft. by 4 ½. Material comes in 9ft. by 4 ½, but you have to have some to lap over, don't you? How about some ideas on this. It's about time my trunk started thinking about getting here. Sure could use that Tupperware for bread, etc. I have a water filter, about 3 gallons of water or so, so I can use what I have for sugar, etc. Can't figure how to hang pictures. The walls are plaster...can't break. I need to get some recipes for things like egg salad. Am about to go have some clothes washed,

Ron Horton

by me, work a little around the house and go for a ride or walk in the Mato (woods).

Whenever I went to the movies in Fatima do Sul or in Dourados, I would be looking down on everyone else's head. I was a good head taller than virtually every one of the residents. The one phenomenal exception was at mid-year conference in Sao Paulo when I got on a hotel elevator, and there were several gorgeous blond women, all taller than me...the traveling Czechoslovakian women's Volleyball team.

December 30, 1966
6:00 pm
Hi,
Can't remember where I left off. I'm in Campo Grande with the PCV's. I am now 23 years old. Got the cards, thanks. Had a big Christmas dinner in the missionary's house here in town, ham, etc. Had turkey yesterday for a combined Birthday party for my boss and me. Fixing cheeseburgers, cole slaw and potato salad. Tomorrow is New Years. I'm going back home Sunday. My trunk is there waiting! Vivian went back yesterday. Got a beautiful silver churasco (steak) knife, with silver sheath from Pat. Am going to get her something though it looks like we're through. Having a nice time, but will be happy to get back home, get my trunk unpacked, get my mail, and get straightened out again. Shaved my mustache for the New Years. Met two volunteers I didn't know. Real cut-ups. Had some good times swimming and at the parties. Have about 15 or more here now. Had about 20.

Health Post-Jan.2, 6:55 am
Received the rest of your cards when I got back. My trunk isn't here. Somewhere between here and Cuiaba. I believe in Dourados. Am going there today to pick up some

malaria medicine and perhaps my trunk. I might go this morning...it looks like today is an election day. Terezinhan isn't here yet and it's ten after.

10:00 pm
Went to Dourados to get my trunk... wasn't there; flies in Thursday (maybe). Going back in then. Vivian was here when I got back. We were both glad to see each other. It's nice having her here. Glad to hear you made contact with Dorothy in Boston. It'll be nice having a guitar to while the hours away.
Got cards from the Vanderburgs, Bill, Jack and Terry, Ann, and I think Clara. We're getting at least two guys and two married couples here in the school this month. Hope I can stay. One couple I know of is an American or Canadian missionary. It'll be nice having them. They have four daughters, all real young. Am going to bed, my love. Congratulate Bill for me. Tell Francis I'll drop her a line.

Love,
Ron

Jan. 2, 1967 2:30 pm
Hi,
Got the birthday card, your taste in cards is really improving. I liked the Christmas card too (the three goons). It really seemed close when you talked about Christmas and Bill and Ann and the group. The gifts in cards are coming through fine. I really appreciate it.

Things are jumping here. Vila Brazil is now using the lab (one day/week) in Dourados, and half the town is looking for a better building for the Health Post. The old auxillar is coming in Monday to go out with me and give me some pointers; but Ron had changed his mind as I think has become apparent, and now would like to work as a lab tech. I was never the door-to-door salesman as I mentioned. Got a card from Dexter the other day.

Oh, my trunk is here. It was shipped to another volunteer in Dourados, so 4 days, two round trip bus rides, 3 carriage rides, and much sweat later, I got it home. Barbosa, (my apartment guy) is in Cuiaba' still. Vivian is here and is in culture shock. Everything Brazilian is wrong for her. She's real bitchy at the moment. Hope she comes out of it. The Tupperware is beautiful! So is the rest of the clothes and fishing tackle (I'm going tomorrow).

How was Natal there, and who won the Super Bowl Game? I'm about to go ask a guy if he wants to go fishing tomorrow and see his folks; they asked me to spend Christmas and New Year with them. They're good people. My next letter will be typed, maybe. Did I pack that small skillet? My trunk was opened at customs, and I'm not sure everything is here, though it appears to be. It's 1967, I'm 23 and in South America! Miss you. How is this thing with Russia and China developing: Let me know. Five weeks to conference. Hope to have trained more by then and have my microscope. My love to all.

Ron

    During Peace Corps training in Milwaukee the veteran PCV's told us to watch out for certain symptoms of not adjusting upon arrival in country like sleeping 24 hours a day, obvious things, and to ease our adjustment, Peace Corps had supplied every PCV with a cardboard book locker with 100 paper back books. Novels, books on Viet Nam, histories. It was amazing how fast I went through mine and soon began to trade with other PCV'S, though I did use the one on Viet Nam as I read on the loo, then used what pages I had just read in an appropriate manner as I finished. There would be 20 or 30 duplicates on the average between lockers, but still I went through 400-500 books.

Time drug by slower than cold molasses on sandpaper; the overall waste of my time and life seemed to be sucking. There were no TV and no radio stations except for BBC at night at Janice's apartment, though I did have a small transistor radio, one of the very first, which I often turned on, but only once during those two agonizingly slow passing years did I pick up a station, and it was some damned missionary; I couldn't figure out from where.

Being an American kid, 23 years old, somewhat shy and essentially unable to speak the language hardly at all, I spent a lot of time by myself after I worked half a day in the Health Post. If I didn't have any Community Development Project going on, I would usually have a couple of caipiringas at lunch between 12:30 and 2:00 and write or simply sit in some outdoor café and watch Brazil go by.

As soon as I would walk up the road to the apartments, there'd be the kids, some on school days or not, usually six or eight. The biggest boys, nine or ten year olds, clad only in homemade cotton shorts with elastic waists, barefoot, looking at everything we Americans did. We were real novelties. The kids in Fatima do Sul who had never had a chocolate candy bar before remain in the smiley part of my brain as they sat in the dirt of their mud and stick houses, beaming like little cherubs as they ate Hershey bars mom had sent me from home. The kids around Janice didn't steal too often, unlike the gangs who "fish-bowled" me in Fatima do Sul. Reading my letters home as I write this, I am amazed how often I was robbed. I don't know how many times my letters mentioned coming home to find all my food and clothes had been stolen again, and me getting paid so little and so rarely or at all by Peace Corps. There always seemed to be kids looking in the doorway, hanging out to play soccer or something; I guess their parents were too busy trying to eke out enough to buy rice and beans. The adults didn't spend much time with the kids who lived around the school in Fatima or at the apartment complex in Dourados.

JAN. 9 7:00 AM

Hi,
Just arrived at the Post, and it looks like I'm very early. My clocks were stopped last night when I arrived home. Went to a fazenda (farm) about 10 kilometers out yesterday at 9:00 am and stayed till about 9:00 last night. The house was of split wood, dirt floor, split tile roof, mud in the cracks inside and out, very clean, and very good people. I went with a German family. We fished in a little creek, played peteca ball, ate oranges, limas (similar to oranges) and some new fruits all day. Had chicken and the meat of a big rodent like animal, capivara, (I thought it was pork until he told me). I saw parrots, parakeets all day long. It took about 30 minutes to drive this six miles. Very rough roads. We were in the jungle. Got home dirty, wet and hungry, with no kerosene and no water in the house. I think Barbosa will be coming in today or fairly soon. Going to talk to the Hospital and Prefectura today about a new post and the laboratory pick-up service. Tomorrow we will pass out the cans for the intestinal parasites and Wednesday I'll collect it here at the Post and put it on the bus.

You would have loved being out with me yesterday; the people were unspoiled, hardworking, country folk. It was beautiful there, dozens of orange trees to keep it cool and green, swept dirt yard, and the house was covered inside with calendars. The German family mentioned another place to go soon. Hope to get Vivian along next time.

Peace Corps Syndrome

It's really going to rain today; it's black as far as you can see in all directions. I'm already dirty (tan jeans) from playing with a dog. I've got a cat coming, and might get one of the dogs in back of the Post, but they're wormy and real bad off. Hope to send you some photos of the town and us in the next week or so. I'm using a camera of an Argentinian, Al B_____, the English speaking guy at whose fazenda I've been a few times. It has all the settings, and I'm not real sure what I'm doing. Have got people looking for a parrot all over. Hope to get one soon. Today I'm going to make posters of some description advertising the lab campaign. Don't know what to say, "Bring your feces in to have it checked?" That doesn't sound too good, but what am I going to say? I must have arrived damn early, still no sign of anyone.

I've got to wash clothes today. I'm out of pants, and it's raining. Think I'll send my pants to the lauandaria (wash woman). It'll save hours of work and she can get them spotlessly clean. Maybe today's a holiday. No one's up and about and it's raining. Maybe we don't open on rainy days.

I'm off. Going to write a few more letters before and if the others arrive. Got a letter to Don in care of you. Would you drop it by his house where Mrs. R__ can forward it? I'm filthy from my notebook too. Everything here has dust or mud on it.
Love,
Ron

Jan. 10, 7:15 am
Just got here again. Made some posters yesterday about the lab pick-up day here with Terezinha's help, and when I got through she gave some flimsy excuses for not

advertising. Vivian and I think she's just anti-change of any sort. This will bring more people in, eventually more personnel and change. She's used to spending two or three hours cleaning the Post because if she doesn't take this long, she has nothing to do for several hours; she's a hard worker, but I think we've got problems. My house is disarranged again, so today is house day. Washed clothes yesterday, planted a few okra, tomato, radish and pumpkin seed.

Vivian is in that book from training in my room. About 5'10", short blond hair. She's in one shot giving injections next to a table. We're getting along well. Thanks again for the stuff to the priest. Terezinha is here.

Bye,
Ron

January 23, 1967 4:30

Hi,
I can't remember when I wrote last, so I thought I'd better

Peace Corps Syndrome

get a letter off. Though I'm penniless, (I have about 450 cruzeiros), just about without cigarettes, and counting minutes till supper, I'm planning to change ten dollars American into cruzeiros, for the purpose of buying an onca. It's an ocelot, like the cat on Honey West. A friend advanced me three mil Saturday and I bought a skin of a young jaguar. Tell Rhonda it's hers when I get home. Oh, Rhonda, thanks for the photo; I have it on my desk; it's the best picture you have made.

We had a Brazilian barbeque yesterday, real good, though I felt bad about not having any money to help buy things; I'm going to give them a dinner or re-pay them. My vacation pay for Christmas still hasn't arrived, along with about 40 mil more the Peace Corps owes me. Vivian went into Campo Grande Friday to talk and help plan our conference, and I hope she'll bring my checks back with her. She should have arrived yesterday afternoon, but isn't here yet. I think she might be coming down with a new PC girl for Vila Gloria, a town about 15 or 20 miles away. I don't think we're going to get any new volunteers here this time; it looks like they're all used up. Janice (Dourados) is coming down for a dinner here, and Rod, perhaps on Sunday. I'd like to go into Cuiaba' for the next three weeks for training until conference, but I haven't heard one word from the Boss in Cuiaba'. If I don't see or hear from someone by tomorrow, I'm going to walk into Campo Grande and hang a few people.

Thanks tremendously for the time, trouble, and money you expended on the packages to the Priest. I've been studying the guitar a little and am ready to practice. How in the world did it come to be twenty pounds? Oh, a package is waiting in the town of Corumba, the entry point for packages. I had to send some stamps for it, all of about 20 cents; and it will take a week longer than it would have,

Ron Horton

since I lost the card I received, and a friendly postmaster had to come to my rescue and pull some jeito.

We have the lab day here now two days per week, though now it's limited to twenty people per day. I can't decide if this is worse or better. I'm going in tomorrow to talk with the head of FUSMAT, the organization I'm with, and perhaps the Governor, if I can get to him, to talk about the Health Post, water, medicines, doctors, I'm hoping we can get direct shipment of supplies here, for they seem to be stopping or used elsewhere when they go through Dourados. I've decided I'll stay here if I can get a microscope, but if I can't in two or three months, I'm going to transfer to another site, perhaps in the Amazon. I would definitely be unhappy here working only as an auxillar. I've just talked myself out; it's about five now, and I think I will walk out in the rain, and kill time before supper. I'm going to see if Vivian comes in on the 6 o'clock bus also. My love to all, tell Ann I just received her Christmas card Friday. Is Don still in school or what? I got a card from Doctor Mount about the possibility of "something" in his department when I get back. I'm very homesick at the moment, and would love to be there.

Love,
 Ron

Feb. 8, 1967 10.30 am

Hi,
Can't remember when I wrote or what I last said, there's been so much confusion lately. Vivian and I are on one meal per day. Still no check. We changed some U. S. money yesterday, half of my Kennedy silver half-dollars for bus fare to conference and cigarettes this week. Six weeks is damned ridiculous for a check to be coming. Particularly

Peace Corps Syndrome

when the last one was 3 ½ months ago. No good news here really. Carnaval is just over. We had a table and drinks on credit till the end of Feb. The people here go crazy for 4 days, drinking and dancing. It's something to see. The rest of the year they're reserved, somber, but lately, gee.

Another kid arrived at the house, forestry this time. We've about got a football team going. One drawback here, my favorite kid robbed me again; I've caught him red handed twice, and told him Wednesday that he couldn't play football till he returned my cards, balls, and Brazilian coins, and 10 minutes later he sneaked in my house, stole my Kool-Aid, bread, and some other things. I've been trying to find him. The other kids are pressuring him after I said no more football for anyone till the things are returned. This might be the wrong approach, but a couple of responsible kids look good to me as they're handling it. This has made me sick. I'm down on several points, but am feeling good and enjoying life, but think I'm going to talk to my boss about a town with a lab. This town is good and is beginning to feel like home, I have friends etc., but with this Health Post and thieves, I'm a little down on it. The lab in Dourados is about to stop our lab worm program and they're getting another doctor. I'm getting angry with the lack of spirit here to fight and/or demand things; water for the Post, medicines, a doctor, a microscope. I'm going to Raise Hell next week with the Chefe of FUSMAT.

Heard from Clara today. She said you were coming over this weekend I think. She had just finished her handi-crafts course. Excuse the dirt on the letter, but there's still no water in the Post here.

As you can see I'm at a low point. Things will be happening this coming week and I'll know what I'm going to do about it. Noe' (my Biology friend) and Vivian's

Ron Horton

Brazilian sister and I have been collecting insects, Butterflies. He's a wonder. Really like him.

Well Mom, thanks for listening to my bitching. I feel better. I'm off to scrape lunch together.
Ron T.

Feb. 19   9:15am

Auntie Dear,
Well I'm off in the morning for Campo Grande and five days of conference, which will be greatly welcomed by this party, as Vivian and I both have been waiting seven weeks for checks, and am smoking rope (the very cheapest tobacco came literally in ½ inch thick rope like coils; you paid by the length) *and am losing weight and my mind.*

Had an ocelot for one week and he escaped. You've probably heard from Mother on this. Danced Carnaval here one night and while recuperating watched the next three. These quiet reserved people go ape for four days, dancing, drinking, and raising hell. I guess it's comparable to Mardi Gras, though I've never seen that gala affair.

My nurse is slowly going out of her tree, and I don't think she will last. Making some good drinking buddies, in fact, I have a house full. I'm getting a missionary family next week, and I hope they don't necessitate my moving. There's one apartment left, and they're coming down for two. With my boss and the State Health Organization wanting me to look at sites that need a lab tech, I think I might consider it, particularly if I'm living in a hotel or Pensao (Ughggh).
Well, give them Hell back there; drink a "Salty Dog" for me, and don't wait till next Christmas to drop me a red letter.

Your Jungle Buddy Nephew,
Ron T.

23 de Marco

Hi,
You're a doll. I got into Dourados Saturday and got my

Ron Horton

packages. It was like Christmas. The Kellogg's Corn Flakes are real good. So are the pens and socks, super balls, sheets, etc., the kitchen things. I'm back in Vila Brazil, leaving tomorrow for Dourados and an Indian mission. Janice and I are going into the Jungle for at least a week to vaccinate, do blood and feces exams. I had just enough time to unpack and repack for the coming week. This is Easter weekend and all the holidays. I might get a day or two fishing before we leave with a new volunteer in Dourados.

I think I owe you several letters. I'm getting the bank thing off today or tomorrow, also my income tax, and catching up on letters. I've been repairing a microscope to use with the Indians. Vivian has just finished a class for Parteiras (Midwives) and is helping another town start a Health Post. The new Chefe we have is swearing to give us a lab and doctor here. I'll believe it when I see it, though I do believe he is serious. I must run to get this in the P.O. Will write from the jungle next week.

*Love,
Ronnie*

Peace Corps' idea was to give us an obvious front into the community, working half a day in the Health Post and then doing what we were really trained for, community development. Spark an idea that was needed for local improvement and then step back and let them think it was their idea. I worked for six to eight months on organizing Boy Scouts and trying to get a source of protein for the protein deficient Indians. Before contact with the Bible toting missionaries, they were the healthiest, happiest people on the planet. Now only a few years after the missionaries had come into the jungle to give them Jesus

Peace Corps Syndrome

and the Bible, they were full of tuberculosis, diphtheria, measles, VD, and were dying like flies. The men were almost all alcoholics, their once macromayed jungle palaces and beautiful dress and crafts exchanged for stick and mud hovels and white men's rags.

My first week in Mato Grosso I was taken to the home of some missionaries in Cuiaba' by an elfish little PCV named Mark, who was working north on the Xingu River with several Indian tribes, the Nambuquari and the Borroro. Before our arrival, he started telling this unbelievable story about two missionaries killed by a tribe hostile to having a seaplane fly into their jungle and that the widows were just now flying back into the same tribe to make contact. Their story had just come out in Reader's Digest. Mark thought the two women might be home, but we soon discovered from the ladies babysitting about five of their kids that the widows were airborne at the moment. So we called them up on their ham radio, and I was introduced to both just before they got to their new site. At that time I was very impressed by these ladies; I was too green a kid to see the wrong being done to these pristine, primitive tribes by Bible toting fanatics stealing the culture, health, and innocence of the Indians. First, contact the poor heathens; shame them into wearing clothes, trade for their macromayed hammocks, hishi bead necklaces, bows, and other crafts for things like mirrors, the common cold, the Bible, schools, measles that wipe out 25 per cent of the tribe and smallpox that wipes out 40 per cent of the people. Bring in others who'll trade them alcohol; then you'll have them hooked on booze, and a couple of them will trade their daughters for a bottle or two. Ah, VD...TB. How unbelievably bitter I find myself now talking about those years, writing about those zealots.

I worked on getting fish ponds dug for the Indian reservation, and raised rabbits to pass out since there was a severe protein deficiency among them. Anyone accepting rabbits, first, had to give two other people a pair before they could be used for food. Janice had hit a dead end in her community projects, and when we heard that dozens of Indian children were suddenly dying from diphtheria in villages to the south, we jumped at the opportunity to go visit these people. We had gone on several such reservation hopping jaunts before, where we had vaccinated the Indians for DPT (diphtheria, pertussis and typhoid) and smallpox, and I had done stool exams for hookworm or roundworm, passing out medicine to the 50-65% positive at most reservations. The missionaries would usually put us up. I slept in several churches in my hammock and on wooden plank church pews.

April 8, 3:00
Hi,
I received your letter and card, also one from Clara telling about Robin C being in the hospital. I've had a halfway legitimate excuse for not writing, constantly traveling, being in strange quarters, not always with stationary, etc. I received the knife and have been aware of its caliber. It's a damn good one, has a very good edge. Had a note from Ann about two weeks ago. I write about every 4 or 5 days, but someone always interrupts, or I lose it in my notebook.

Just got in from the Indian Post in Amambai with an Army Jeep and driver at our disposal for the weekend. Had to come in for vaccine, the film projector, and some (pardon) ass here who somehow got our machine told me I had to have written permission to get it. The Chefe brought it down for us. We're working on it. Things are looking up. I'm working hard, getting a lot done, over 100 exams, vaccinated 50. Not spending any money to speak of, and still have more than a month's pay coming in. I'm actually in good financial shape. Still healthy too. We're staying with a Presbyterian missionary in Amambai. I was sleeping

Peace Corps Syndrome

in the one room church in a hammock with a horse blanket as cover. We have rice and beans, beans and rice, and orange and rice to eat. All the native fruits are ripening and we have some oranges, tangerines, some fruit like a plum that we can eat. The Indians are living worse than when the whites began to attempt to civilize them. It's really pitiful. Dirty, sick, wormy, etc. I appreciate the clippings and cards you send, put most of them up on the wall. Haven't heard from Don, Jesslyn or anyone. So say hi to everyone you see. I broke up with the girl here. Well, I'm off to catch up on the rest.

*Love,
Ron*

One time we lucked up as the Brazilian government had a national medical group that had just arrived from Rio de Janeiro with a double mission to all the Indian villages; they were x-raying and treating tuberculosis for one, and they also had a dental team with them. Janice and I met this crew from Rio when they dropped by the Health Post. They were spending a few days at the Guarani Indian village north of Dourados where Janice and I worked occasionally.

Thirty minutes after meeting them we had talked them into letting us travel with them as they toured other Guarani and Borroro tribes. The Health Post doctors and the new government crew worked with us, and we soon had a large quantity of DPT vaccine, smallpox vaccine, and other gear packed for Janice and for me. I also took along my microscope, hand powered centrifuge, glass slides and stain for doing blood exams, and my platinum loop to skim hookworm and roundworm eggs off the surface of watered stool specimens after I flung them around at several hundred RPM, just inches from my face, while cranking my centrifuge.

Ron Horton

The Rio crew was a wild and funny group. Most had done their medical training in the States and spoke better English than we spoke Portuguese. We all went to an outdoor restaurant, the Figueira, for supper and drinks. Food at these places was always delayed on purpose for about an hour to allow the customers' time to visit and drink. The waiters first bought little ten-inch loaves of bread; for hor d'oeuvres you poured some olive oil into the center of your plate, then some vinegar from the little jars always on Brazilian tables right into the center of the oil so that it looked like a raw egg. We'd tear off a piece of the hard crusted, white bread and dip it into the oil-vinegar mix. Ah, those big Brazilian beers. The head dentist made fun of my redneck Portuguese by talking to me in redneck English. We sat at a big round table under a fig tree which had once been a giant in the jungle among other ancient monarchs.

The dentists and doctors were great folks, and Janice and I had a blast traveling with them. We traveled in Toyota four-wheel-drive station wagons, along with two decent trucks, one with a big aluminum trailer carrying the X-ray equipment. Just outside town, we had to pull over for twenty minutes or so while a cattle drive of several thousand, driven to market from hundreds of miles away, crossed the road. The herd was being managed by about eight cowboys who were decked out head to toe in leather with strange little squished leather helmets. One Cavalheiro had a five-foot horn so long that it seemed to be impossible to be from any animal living on earth. He blew only two signals; "Let's go" and "Stop", consisting of a bunch of hoots or a long steady hoot. There was a string of horses, led by the cook, carrying thick leather trunks loaded with their grub. The cowboys carried stiff, three strand, braided lariats in case they needed them for the herd, mainly Brahmas and a few beautifully striated zebu cattle, their backs covered in dozens of one inch high, pus-oozing, blow-fly larva filled, open sores. The herd completely blocked the narrow muddy lane that wound between dense jungles on either side. They spooked at the vehicles moving ahead until finally we had to stop completely while three of the Cavalheiros scurried the steers around us.

When we arrived at the first Indian village at about 10:30 in the morning, seemingly millions of butterflies on the banks of a small river sprang up in giant fantasies of strobe-like color shifts as we splashed through in our vehicles. Thatch covered pole buildings dotted the half savannah, half jungle; the biggest was up a little red dirt road on a knoll where two or three hundred Indians were gathered. The men were mostly wearing cotton shorts; only a few wore shirts while the women wore old rags. I was amazed when a quarter of a century later I read my own letters describing them as filthy and really pathetic figures, lots of children with Kwashikora extended stomachs.

In 2002, having just watched a Discovery Channel special on the Xingu tribe north of Cuiaba', I reveled at their healthy, happy grins as they played in their immaculate villages. But forty years ago these Indian tribes a few hundred miles to the south had nothing at all; most of the game that they had lived on was gone, victim to the cancerous subsistence farmers who have to move every few years as the tropical forest soils are almost totally lacking in nutrients. Slash and burn. I heard a lot of stories about Indians being slaughtered for their land by big ranchers in particular; one story told of a rancher with a machine gun and small plane chasing a tribe off their lands north of Alto Paraguay.

The villagers told us that they had lost 12 children between this village and another to diphtheria. My grandmother, Annie Laurie Shaw, had the disease in the U.S. around the turn of the last century and had told me how horrible it could be, the incessant coughing to clear the phlegm that never allowed a breath. The whole medical group set up on one side of the big tribal center, a large roofed, open barn like building; the tuberculosis people with their diesel generated X-ray soon had suspected and known cases of the dreaded disease stretched out around the corner in a long line. Months later when I was having my medical exam on leaving Brazil, I had a positive skin test for TB, but never came down with the disease. Many of the Indians with TB had received antibiotics only long enough to partially recover without actually killing the bacterium, and so their infection was now immune to all medication. This is the exact reason for the resurgence of tuberculosis worldwide in a new virulent, untreatable form. We didn't realize at the time just how deadly contagious these cases were.

Indians with bad teeth formed an even longer line for the dentists. While I watched in amazement, the dentist would push the snaggle-toothed people into his chair, take a five second look as he injected Novocain into their mouths, and begin snatching out rotten teeth. He would literally service each patient in less than five minutes, often pulling four or five teeth. Janice and I established our station on the far side of the tribal hut.

Soon we were surrounded by hundreds of Indians; Janice showing her usual magic with the children as we injected and poked them for vaccinations. They stretched around the corner in a long line. Only the men spoke any Portuguese, the women rattling on in Guarani or whatever. With our gear stretched out on a crude wooden table with bamboo legs, Janice and I began handling the ragtag Indians who formed a line of several hundred. While one of us injected DPT vaccine in one arm, the other vaccinated the opposite arm for smallpox. For the latter procedure we used, just as we had hundreds of times before back at our Health Post or at other Indian villages, two-and-a-half-inch long sterilized brads or nails. You had to grab their arm, holding the nail like a short spear, and jab 20 or 30 times.

Peace Corps Syndrome

Our colleagues back at the Health Post were so childlike that when we were doing smallpox vaccinations there one or two would laughingly insist on re-vaccinating us and poke us several times with the sharp nails.

Only a few years later the World Health Organization claimed that smallpox was wiped out from the earth. Janice and I had a neighbor, less then a block away from where we lived on the main dirt highway, whose daughter worked in a butcher's shop while she had an active case of smallpox. The local health officials knew about her, but never closed the shop. A very typical, Brazilian-type occurrence. Every day one could see ten to twenty people suffering with jungle rot, their nasal septums completely gone from this form of the disease. These jungle folks were accustomed to seeing open sores.

The second day was set aside for intestinal parasite exams. Word had been passed to the Indian tribe to bring in small samples of their poop. I had done hundreds of such tests back in Dourados, particularly with school kids, and they never tested less than 85% positive for hookworm and roundworm. Doctors estimated that such severe infestations could cause a person to lose as much as a pint of blood a day to these enormous worms, some up to a foot long. The Brazilians would bring their stool samples in small glass containers or some similar container provided by the Health Post. Nothing prepared me for the onslaught of Indian containers. For this occasion they demonstrated their thousands of years of crafting from nature. As each man, woman, or child came in under the thatch roof and gave Janice their name, they would hand me their stool samples, each individually wrapped in everything from cow horns to small gourds, all hand crafted with macramé or stitched with vines. There were leaves intricately stitched with grasses, bark containers bound with leather, animal horns bound in leather. Janice and I both felt like we were really accomplishing something for the first time in our

Ron Horton

Peace Corps career, saving lives and doing some real good.

We made several trips with the Brazilian National group before they left for Rio. While Janice and I were doing this work, Peace Corps had forgotten to pay us again for almost four months and both of us had to draw on our PC "savings" money which we sent home and our folks would then have to try to smuggle back to us. We both felt the need was so great and acute that we used what very little money we had to finance our expeditions. I had to resort to smoking tobacco in rope form again, buying it by the foot. You had to shave it into small flakes and then roll it. It was so damn potent that though I smoked over two packs of Camels a day, the first time I tried one of those rope cigarettes I was reeling drunk from the effects after only two or three draws.

Once while Janice and I were on one of the Mercedes Benz buses typical to South America, a particularly long bus ride to the east to another small frontier village where a missionary was to meet us and drive us to the Indian village in the jungle, we were squirming in our seats. We had drunk a big beer just before leaving and the bus hadn't stopped in almost two hours. Janice was looking green and said, "God, if they don't stop soon, I'm going to be in real trouble." The better bus stops had actual restrooms, but the toilets didn't have seats, as the local custom was to stand on the sides of the commode and squat, leaving red mud footprints during the rainy season.

She was the third out when the bus actually stopped and a line formed for the single privy. Many of the passengers, particularly mothers with four or five children, simply walked twenty or thirty feet into the treelessness of the savannah, dropped to a squat and went to the bathroom. I was just behind her as she finally got to stop wiggling and entered the one-seater outhouse. Just then I noticed that the privy was on skids, the bottom open to chickens and pigs. Nothing was wasted. When Janice came out there was a

Peace Corps Syndrome

squabble of chickens, and immediately behind me as I unzipped, the fastest chicken ran at full tilt pursued by three or four more fat chickens out of my view. I heard some laughter behind me as I came out and walked back into the crowd of passengers; the alpha chicken ran right through the middle of us holding a bright red Tampax. Janice was running for the bus.

We found the missionary waiting for us, and again we found that Indian children had been dying like flies; whooping cough they called it. We stayed three or four days doing all that we could do, vaccinating and doing parasite exams. Much to our chagrin when we returned to Dourados, the new Mato Grosso Peace Corps director showed up ranting and raving. "Where the hell have you been; you're supposed to be at the Health Post. When we explained what the two of us had been doing with the Indian village, saving possibly hundreds of lives that would not have been saved if we had not acted, Butch D_____ was not impressed. He demanded that we return to the Health Post in Dourados where in 1968 we were not needed. Another fucking bureaucrat! In Peace Corps no less, what a jerk! They used Janice at a desk at the Health Post shoving papers. And even though there were now two other lab techs beside myself, we were forced to stop our work with the Indians. Butch strutted out to his Willys and drove off into further acts of stupidity, I'm sure, while Janice and I sank into a drinking lethargy. By now we had several good friends at the Health Post, and though they were quite friendly, no amount of commiseration could help.

It was during this madness that, as previously mentioned, all of our cats and animals mysteriously died, and I had to give Janice most of the rabies shots after she diagnosed it as probable "insipid" rabies, a variant form. And there was suddenly a new Peace Corps couple who arrived and moved into the same apartment complex, but they cracked up pretty fast and shipped out to the States. We partied hard after coming in from the Health Post or after bicycling in from the Indian village. Earlier PCV's had Willys Jeeps, but in their infinite wisdom, one of our Peace Corps directors felt that bicycles made a better statement. Bicycling in the tropical sun, through dust storms in the dry season and impassable mud holes in the rainy season when it came down in torrents every day, was simply too damned hard. There was less and less for us to do as time went by and our tours began to wind down. Janice and I became so platonically close that we acted like brother and sister. I was too much of a kid for her to consider me a man, but I developed a horrible crush on her. Nothing sexual or romantic ever happened between us.

We sank into a state of mind that was close to insanity. We were only paid every two months and then only forty-five or fifty dollars per month. They paid us the average pay of the impoverished Brazilian pioneer. Just at this low point, the main office got screwed up again and forgot about paying us for almost four months. This was the second time we had not received our salary; 10,000 miles from home without food, family or friends to help us, it got really weird. When family in the US sent money through the mail, it was stolen by postal employees. All incoming mail was opened and looted. Once again we were reminded of the story that when the main Post Office in Rio got behind, they simply took a large boatload of mail off the coast and sank it, after looting it of course. Janice had the idea to glue the larger greeting cards together so money could be sealed inside. I sold my typewriter and we scrimped by.

Janice had met an Argentine-English rancher in Campo Grande several months before and danced with him at a party at Dr. Bill's house. One afternoon while Janice and I were in her apartment, Al pulled up in front of her door, suntanned, wearing a funky cowboy hat with a cool,

Peace Corps Syndrome

feathered hatband. I could feel the attraction between them as he talked. He asked us to come up to his ranch for a few days saying, "I'll bring y'all back in a coupla days." We jumped at the chance to be well fed and were ready to go within minutes. His ranch was about three hours to the north, toward Maracaju over the rough, red dirt roads. I was in the back seat of his VW van called a Kombi when he hit a particularly big bump, probably while he was trying to look down Janice's loose cotton pullover. I flew through the air landing on my left hand, and to my horror my left ring finger was bent sideways. Just as I thrust it toward Janice hollering, "Put traction on it," my finger popped back into alignment by itself. By the time we arrived at the ranch house my finger was grotesquely purple and swollen.

Al's ranch was a Swiss owned and designed showpiece that was crossing Santa Gertrudis and Charolais cattle with the native Brahma. The water system on the ranch was perhaps the most ingenious thing I had seen to date on earth. A spring behind the house was captured in a four foot wide, one-foot-deep concrete trough that approached the house and turned by the back bedrooms, the only side of the house without 15 foot wide porches with hammocks and chaise lounges everywhere. As it turned and came beside the house, it passed through a water ram, an ancient mechanical device with a piston that very slowly pumped out about one percent of the water that passed through it, up ten-feet to a water storage box above the bathroom. Thirty-feet later, the water trough turned and entered the house making a 15 foot u-shaped turn about the kitchen. The water flowed over dishes in racks and over other racks holding fresh vegetables. Just as the water exited the kitchen it cascaded into a 25 foot long log hollowed into a giant spoon shape. The spoon was six feet long and three feet wide, two-and-a-half to three feet deep. The handle was long and narrow and went through a tall rectangular slit in the block wall of a separate room. In that room the end of the spoon was attached to a six-foot tall dangling mortar above an enormous rice filled pestle. Every Brazilian household had smaller devices in the back yard for de-husking rice.

When the spoon part of the device filled with water, it would fall, spilling water and raising the arm in the other room. When it was empty, the balance of the arm was such that the wooden spoon would then rise back up to be filled. The wooden pole in the other room would smash down into a ten gallon wooden bowl filled with fresh dried rice still in its husks. Every thirty minutes or so, one of the cooks would change the rice, taking what had been smashed from its husks outside in a three-foot flat straw basket. They would toss the rice high in the air, the wind blowing the husks away while the rice fell back into the two-inch deep basket. This much rice was necessary for the 10-12 cowboys and their families who lived in nice cabins out back of the gardens.

I would visit Al's ranch many times and often helped him move cattle around the ranch. He had some really beautiful breeds. He also had a big string of horses, and I would usually get a really spirited cow-pony. Once we were moving all his Brahma bulls, along with one old, real mean critter who had been partly crippled fighting with the other bulls. He really didn't want to get up from his shady repose; I had to charge him three times before he got up, really pissed off, and charged me. Good horse.

The first day at Al's ranch with Janice was a hoot. We had a barbeque and some of the beef ribs must have been four-feet long. After we ate, we stretched out in hammocks on the porches and watched the sunset. Janice and Al dropped into one hammock and after several drinks, they began to snuggle, so I went around the corner and soon on to my room. I lit the lamp to read awhile and just as I was turning it off, an hour or so later, I began to hear sounds

Peace Corps Syndrome

from through the wall right behind my bed. Even over the din of 30 billion insects and half that many frogs calling for girlfriends, I could hear Janice moaning and talking. Oh god, I thought, I'm hearing Janice lose her 35-year-old virginity. Soon she was moaning with every breath, about two seconds apart, then one second apart, and then she shouted, "Oh god, oh god," three or four times. I put my pillow over my head. I wanted to die. All the times I had dreamed about making love to her and now this. Even with the pillow over my head and five million mosquitoes buzzing outside my mosquito net, fifty million crickets chirping and other critters chirping, I could hear her. I think she must have had an orgasm from her increasing moans and gasps, for she was relatively quiet for a few minutes. Then I started to hear the bed creaking and the headboard hitting the wall inches away from my head now turned toward her. If my arm had been long enough and magical, I could have reached out and stroked her. Soon she began a long wailing, "Al, Al, baby, baby," each time the bed post hit the wall. Their bed springs were squeaking like a rusty factory. Al was long winded and the sounds went on and on. Janice gasping and moaning just inches away.

It was pure anguish. I was going crazy and what a boner! It must have drained all the blood out of my brain. So now as I tossed and turned, my erection demanded attention, thinking about her freckled breasts and dappled thighs, the pitch of her moans and gasps rising till I was like that crazed Brahma bull. I lay there in the dark wishing that it were me on top of all that pent up passion; Janice driven to a sexual frenzy. I was now as sexually excited as I had ever been in my 23 years and imagining what she was doing making all those sounds, seeing her beside me, time was transfixed as my bed began to vibrate. The pain from my broken finger throbbed like crazy as on and on she gasped, sometimes shouting, totally wanton, as her crescendo built, all that just beyond my reach and sight, yet light years away. A dog began to bark from all the noise and commotion adding to the insanity. I think I almost ripped my penis off, I was so crazy. All three of us must have climaxed at about the same time for suddenly it was quiet and time stood still.

I'll never forget the look on her face the next morning. She glowed like a shooting star. Her eyes sparkling, mesmerized by Al, bald as a boiled egg, one arm slightly deformed. That very night the three of us harvested about 40 acres of soybeans that Al had grown for the very first time on the ranch for cattle feed. By the time he figured they were ripe, the beans were so dry that when he pulled his old corn harvester through them most of the beans wound up on the ground. Somehow, he talked Janice and me into helping him harvest them after midnight when the nightly dew and lower temperature would let them be harvested without losing so many, so we stayed up drinking gin and tonic on the patio until midnight.

Al drove the tractor while Janice and I rode in the harvester hopper shoving the soybeans to the back as they poured into the front of the machine. As the machine filled and the soybeans covered first our feet and then our legs, Janice and I would fall and wallow around, twisting our bodies as we used our arms and legs to stroke the beans to the back where they wouldn't fall back over the incoming geyser falling on top of us. She and I were persistently touching and brushing our bodies together by accident, dripping sweat and dust, both moaning as we breathed in almost sheer exhaustion, pushing our bodies to the limit. For hours we stood knee deep and deeper in the beans, thighs touching. A hundred times she fell across me or on top of me. A hundred times I fell across her dripping wet cotton clothes. Our bodies turning in sensuous half turns and thrusts as we struggled to bring in the crop; her cotton covered, sweat drenched breasts brushed and smashed my

Peace Corps Syndrome

chest hundreds of times that night, yet I never purposely touched her, but my body knew hers in a constant frontal embrace. Al was about ten feet away, his beans shooting out of the harvester all over Janice and me.

Al was never serious about Janice and eventually dumped her. He had been shacking up with another Peace Corps nurse from Campo Grande, and I soon learned that he was also dating the daughter of a million acre ranch, partly owned by Winthrop Rockefeller, the Governor of Arkansas. I don't know how Janice found out about his philandering, which was kind of the norm for sexual mores at the time; after all, I slept with four Peace Corps ladies in my last few weeks in Rio later that year. Janice took Al's lack of attention at least outwardly in a lackadaisical manner, but at the same time she started drinking more, just as I was also beginning to do the same. As we got crazier and crazier while we were partying and the urge to tinkle struck us at the same time, we would sometimes race to the bathroom, the first to get drawers down and tinkle, the winner. Once it was a tie and we peed at the same time. I peed standing up at the same time that she peed sitting on the john. My aim was true, somehow, as I swayed, holding my penis a foot from her face, my stream inches from her freckled thighs and her reddish-blond bush.

At times we had little to eat and began to drink cheaper and cheaper booze. The Brazilian corn liquor was only ten cents American. One night there was nothing to mix into our drinks but an old package of JELLO. It started to congeal as we drank it down. The last night Janice was in Brazil I went to Campo Grande to give her one of our typical going away parties for the flight to Rio which left just after dawn each day. We always had a champagne sendoff for our friends, knowing we'd probably never see each other again. So we partied hard at Dr. Bill's the night before. Martinis brewed in Bill's big aluminum pot with his usual one drop of vermouth for the driest martini in Brazil.

In the wee hours when all 12-15 of us Peace Corps Volunteers were partied out, we crashed on Bill's beds, couches, and hammocks. I wound up with four or five in Bill's second bedroom. We were all mostly clothed...as clothed as most Peace Corps parties wound up. But Janice had on shorts and a top, and I had on jeans in the tropical night. At first she and I faced each other in the dark, our faces touching at times as we nestled in, then she turned and faced the other way; I wiggled over just as she waggled her butt. I snuggled closer into her back but had no place for my arm, so I reached across her to find a place. My hand fell on her breast; cupping the soft freckledness felt like touching magic I tingled so much. She reached up and moved my hand away.

The next morning as usual at these going away parties, someone yelled at first light, and we all ran to the Willys Jeeps. I grabbed one of Janice's bags, her trunks having gone before. The plane was early and after only two or three glasses of champagne, I blinked, and she was running for the plane. Almost immediately she was rising into the rosy pink sunrise, the morning flights of parrots off to the side screaming in protest. I never saw nor heard from her again, though over the years I sent a postcard to the address of one of her friends in Boston. In my heart when I think of her, I fear she stumbled back into her Boston trap and never loved another man after Al. Something in me tells me that she probably wound up childless...and her with that perfect mother heart.....AND ALL THOSE FRECKLES!

BRAZILIAN DISEASES AND THE WATER

Suffice to say that Brazil, with virtually every natural resource on earth, also has virtually every disease known to

Peace Corps Syndrome

the planet plus. During Peace Corps training we were taught that the only way to shower was to put some iodine into a glass of water, take a sip and keep it in your mouth, otherwise you'd catch hepatitis, cholera, giardia (which I didcatch), all kinds of intestinal parasites; Schistosomiasis and Chaga's disease were the two most mentioned in training.

Schisto is caused by a microscopic critter that burrows into your skin when you wade, swim, or even wash your hands where it exists; then it burrows on in and becomes a liver fluke, a fatal disease. Chagas is another, then incurable disease, caused by the reduvid or "kissing bug," a critter that lives in cracks or crevices much like a roach, comes out at night and bites people on their lips (its saliva contains an anesthetic and an anticoagulant, so you don't feel it), the softest spot, feeds until it's sated, defecates and leaves. Later when it itches and you scratch it in your sleep, you rub the eggs from their feces into the wound. Voila, Chaga's disease. Almost everybody had intestinal worms, hookworm or ascaris. Daily I would see people without a nasal septum caused by one of the diseases called jungle rot. We, PCV's, took tablets with quinine to ward off malaria, but it caused us to turn yellow, so most of us drank quinine water with gin to ward off the disease.

I caught *Giardia lambia* (an intestinal parasite) two or three times which was hard to distinguish from my usual diarrhea. I had it so bad I had to go into Campo Grande and see Dr. Bill to get some opiate; that seemed to be the only thing to actually stop it. I was doing fecal exams every day at the lab where I would usually open a dozen or so jars of stool samples, take a dab, mix it in water in a test tube, and using a hand cranked centrifuge, sling four open topped vials around at several hundred RPM just inches from my face and mouth. I was so paranoid that I was contaminating myself that I checked myself at least once a week. One day I had an *Amoeba histolytica* (the bad one) egg in my stool exam, the one that can form abscesses in your brain or liver, but miraculously it never showed up again. A good number of my friends who lived out in the jungle had contracted malaria at one time or another. Seu Loide had leprosy before I met him, and once a case of jungle rot showed up at my door. One of Janice's little girls one day asked me to take a look at her brother. It seems he had an infection for about a year and a half; the wound had gotten so big that he had not been able to work in over a year. So a little later she showed up with her 30-year-old brother. I could smell his leg before he unwrapped it. He told me he had gone to the Health Post a year before where they put a dressing on it. Somehow, I correctly deduced he had a massive secondary infection over Leishmaniasis, a form of jungle rot. I wrote a note for him to give to the doctor at the Health Post, and a few months later he had been properly treated and had recovered. They had to treat the secondary infection separately from the jungle rot.

Tuberculosis was everywhere, many cases untreatable because they had only partially killed the bacterium with antibiotics not taken long enough. Serious shit! Actually, one of the most common ailments was Kwashikora where children had grotesquely extended bellies, the classic symptom of protein deficiency. Most had only bread for breakfast, a little rice and black beans later in the day. I knew lots of people who worked for less than one dollar a day, farm hands who ate only twice a day, black beans and rice with a little sun jerked beef thrown in, and they worked from first light to last light.

There were subsistence farmers' mud and stick hovels everywhere, giant jungle hardwoods smoldering through what looked like storm damage, a few stalks of corn popping up here and there being ravaged by flocks of smaller green parrots with yellow topknots, toucans and macaws thrown in for color. Every clearing creates perfect habitat for malaria carrying mosquitoes. The farmers might have an axe, a hoe or two and a few pots and pans. Ragged clothes and homemade sandals made out of old car tires for soles and leather straps. That was it! Most families had at least 6-8 kids and 10-12 were common thanks to the Catholic dominated government that made it illegal to promote birth control. Thanks, Pope. The 30-year-old women often had varicose veins the size of a small anaconda. They were worn out and spent.

The mercury poisoning from the gold mining along the streams in northern Mato Grosso was not apparent then. On the way out of Brazil I heard a colleague from my training group, Dr. Bill Pope, showed a positive for Schistosomiasis. God, what a great team he and his wife, Fran, were.

BUREAUCRATIC BULL SHIT

After being kidnapped by what turned out to be a Peace Corps director of the state of Mato Grosso who thought he needed a lab tech, but actually only needed therapy in peter-principal-ology, I spent the first six to eight months in Brazil spinning my wheels, assigned to a site without a lab, nurses, or doctors. Total bull shit and within two months that asshole left and returned to the States after screwing up my life.

In those first months on site I worked or pretended to work in a fairly new town building, what they called a Health Post; the only thing accomplished here was to give a local woman a place to sit a few hours each day. Nothing related to health care ever went on there, and when I arrived and tried to set up a lab, starting at first with a laboratory specimen service where I would draw samples and bus them into the lab in Dourados once or twice a week, I was opposed. This politically appointed woman refused to allow me to advertise to the town folk in Fatima do Sul to come to the Health Post even though there was no other health care available for the people, except for the very few who could afford to travel four to eight hours to doctors and hospitals.

Hookworm, the big roundworm Ascaris and Amoeba were pandemic, almost 100% of the population tested positive for these parasites resulting in general malaise and lethargy in the already undernourished majority of folks. My Portuguese was still very bad when I attempted to do a city wide health survey. I'd go up to a house and knock; if anyone answered, it was usually the lady of the house in the middle of the day, and I'd say, "Hello, I work for the Health Post, blah blah," and try to ask a few questions about any diseases in the family like malaria, but I used the wrong twang on the verbs, and they always thought that I was asking them if they worked at the Health Post. They were all quite friendly as each replied that, "No, they had never worked at the Health Post."

Lots of wasted time really weighed on me. I really wanted to help in some way but seemed stymied by bureaucrats wherever I turned. It was almost like catching a disease called "Bureaucracy." Once I had contracted this bug, it hung on with a tenacious grip and almost proved to be fatal. It was definitely a reoccurring ailment, and would drive me to desperation in 1968 when a new brat of a Mato Grosso Peace Corps director pulled Janice and me out of the Indian reservations. He was personally responsible for the deaths of untold numbers since they were not being vaccinated for Diptheria, pertussis, tetanus, smallpox, or treated for internal parasites.

COMMUNITY DEVELOPMENT

Our Peace Corps group, which just happened to be the

Peace Corps Syndrome

first all medical team in the Peace Corps, was also a community group. We had received a lot of training in community development. Our medical work was to be our "in" into the community where we would germinate seeds of change, i.e., fish ponds, new wells, privy slabs, cooperatives, Boy Scout troops and then sit back and watch the natives that we inspired carry the idea to fruition. This seemed so rational and sane at the time...that a 23-year-old American could come in and have any ideas worth a squat, or a real understanding of the entire picture, and could initiate anything worth even one of the white, one-cruzeiro bank notes....it required two hundred to buy a box of matches.

Twenty five years later in graduate school, I learned about the horribly detrimental, world changing results which came from such naïve and foolish "Ugly American" know it alls when I read about how the World Health Organization, with all good intentions, had for decades drilled wells in the Sahara and across North Africa for the waterless people and had changed the climate of the earth, i.e. caused the desertification of tens of thousands of square miles in the Sahel of Africa. Tribes like the Masai and others migrated north and south each year with the seasonal rains and coincidentally along with the wilderbeasts. They went where and when the short grasses in the north and the tall grasses in the south grow, as the seasonal rains shift, just as they have for millennia. When good intentioned UN workers drilled wells, the people with their cattle congregated around the wells and quickly denuded the grasses down to bare earth in a short time, yet they stayed because there was water even though they had to drive their cattle further and further to graze.

This resulted in the death of most of their livestock and resulted in more starvation. Thousands of vast denuded circles can now be seen by satellite, and literally the world's climate has been impacted and millions of Africans starve by aiding in the cessation of their north-south annual migration. Barbed wire international borders that further impact this problem is a direct result of less migration by the tribes. Good intentions have caused more misery than if nothing had ever been done. Only after six years in graduate school in the 1980's and 90's, studying ecology, did I fully realized that any Peace Corps Volunteer or international worker should be required to be absolutely schooled in the local ecology before they can ever arrive in country.

I got involved in several projects during my two years, from working organizing Boy and Girl Scout state workers, to organizing Scout troops where I was, working pouring key hole privy slabs to prevent hookworm and other intestinal parasites, raising rabbits as brood stock and trying to raise tilapia fish as protein for the Guarani Indians. Most of the work I did in the Medical lab was the fecal exams for intestinal worms and blood work for malaria or tuberculosis. Brazil averages over a half million cases of malaria a year. I never had less than 85% positives for hookworm or roundworm in the school kids I tried to focus on in my work. Most Brazilian frontier people had no outhouse or privy, even wealthy families by Mato Grosso standards with thousands and thousands of acres of land, vast herds of cattle, and town houses pooped in the pineapple patches out back. I discovered this fact one morning visiting a ranch after asking the lady of the house about the privy; she pointed to the pineapple patch, and I had no choice.

A privy or outhouse could be made by supplying privy slabs. A key-hole privy slab could be made by digging a three to four inch deep hole, about three feet by three feet. Concrete mixed with dirt and a few scrap pieces of wire or metal thrown in for structural strength resulted in a key-hole privy slab. A wooden key-hole design was put in the middle before mixing the concrete. When we wanted to

Peace Corps Syndrome

impress someone, we would build up two raised foot pads to each side of the widest part of the hole just where one would squat while defecating into a hole dug in the ground. Relocate when full, put up walls and a roof if possible; if not, it still kept the parasitic eggs from hatching on the ground where barefooted or bare-ankled folk had the microscopic hookworm larva lurking on blades of grass, ready to jump and burrow into the skin before entering the bloodstream. We made quite a few of those privy slabs.

My colleague and I both went out to the Guarana Indian reservation every chance we had. The mission head, Donna Francisca, had arrived about eight years before when the Indians were still unspoiled, i.e., healthy, happy and living almost idyllic lives in the pristine jungle. Unlike their more isolated and thus luckier brothers to the north, like the now world famous Xingu, who are now protected on Brazilian national preserves and who have maintained their original and idyllic culture and lives, this tribe had a missionary arrive, befriend them, begin to trade and learn their language. She built a post and in no time, common colds, measles, tuberculosis, and smallpox had decimated hundreds.

When we arrived in 1966, they had dozens of cases of tuberculosis of which six to eight were cases of incurable TB, the result of the Indians going off their antibiotics before they were totally cured. I did a positive skin test for TB for years after visiting the ward several times. The trade Donna Francisca started with the tribe quickly bought access to more trade and then booze and alcoholism, and by 1966, their homes had gone from beautiful huts, macramé hammocks and beautiful crafts, to where there was only a small percentage of the people still alive. It appeared most or all of the men were alcoholics, but at least five or six had read eleven pages of the Bible Donna Francisca was translating.

God bless missionaries. There needs to be a special

place in hell for all good intentioned religious zealots. I still remember the first lesson in her language book that she had written. "O uh pah tapiti," or here comes the rabbit, unless you changed the emphasis of the syllables and then you were asking, "Is the rabbit coming?"

The Guarani Indians were pitifully malnourished and hungry. Most of the kids had the extended bellies indicating Kwashikora. My second year I set out to try to get some fish ponds dug by the county road crews to grow tilapia fish as a protein source. Of course, I never realized the contempt of many Brazilians toward the indigenous peoples. Thirty years later, in 1996, while teaching Biology at the University of Montevallo in Alabama, an article in the *Birmingham News* caught my eye and I pinned it to the wall of my office: **"Guarani Indians of Mato Grosso with highest suicide rate on earth**," particularly with the young girls. The government had tricked the Indians into trading their timber to buy farm machinery to turn them into farmers. When the non farming, diseased, and now alcoholic farmers failed, the government clear cut the Guarani's jungle, mostly virgin exotic hardwoods. In other words, they stole their jungle. Suicide among early teenage Guarani is the highest in the world at this moment.

So when my aquaculture Tilapia fish raising project wasn't going anywhere, I bought some rabbits, built two double cages and began to raise protein. After a few months of building pens and fighting off one army ant invasion, I began to give away a male and female rabbit to anyone who would promise to give away two breeding pairs before they ate any.

Early on in 1966, some Lion's Club locals asked me to join their country club; they actually had a steam room, sauna and swimming pool, but I couldn't afford it, and I was too young and dumb to be a big league smaltzer. However, there was always some project going on. The locals had no concept of the "germ theory," so I rounded up the Peace Corps, gas-driven, electric generators and projectors. Peace Corps had great Walt Disney films with Goofy and Mickey Mouse about the germ theory. It is impossible to stop most diseases until folks understand how they catch them. I showed these films every chance I got, and droves of kids would come out with their folks since most could not afford to go to the cinema and most had never seen a projector or cartoons.

There was one hilarious event with the Guarani during the few weeks I had the use of a Willys Jeep. As mentioned before, Early Peace Corps Volunteers had Willys Jeeps, but all we had were bicycles. Some fucking bureaucrat decided our group didn't need vehicles since it might look bad. Doh! Anyhow, one day an American kid showed up saying he was on a Rotary Club fellowship as a linguist and wanted me to take him out to the reservation. About ten days later, oddly enough, another American on a Lion's Club fellowship showed up as well; hell, maybe they were both C.I.A. for all I know, claiming to be doing a photographic pictorial of the different Indians. So, I was showing the second guy around the reservation when we met the Rotary linguist, who was already speaking better Guarani than the Indians. The photographer was trying to shoot the villagers and particularly the women and children. The men tended to congregate along the roads or paths in crude little lean-tos; I guess to do trades for booze; the women were back in the jungle around the thatch shacks.

Every time the photographer would approach the women, they would run into the jungle or into their houses. He failed time after time as we drove around until we ran into the linguist who immediately started teaching him some phrases to say to the women. He told the photo guy, "Say this and they'll pose for you. I'm going to teach you to say, 'Please, I want to take your picture'". That they had no idea what a photo was didn't occur to me, as the linguist said, "Che jahata qua ru." The photographer practiced this phrase several times as the three of us drove into the middle of the reservation in the old tan Willys until we saw another group of women and children. The camera guy jumped out walking toward the group. "Che ja hata qua ru," he said, like John Smith meeting Pocahontas, whereupon the women fell down on the ground laughing uncontrollably. The guy was able to take all the shots he wanted, though the women had no idea what a camera was anyhow.

We did this three times before the linguist turned to me as the photographer walked toward a group and had them laughing like few people I had ever seen before. "You know what he's saying?" "No," I replied. He grinned and said, "He's saying, I've got to take a piss". This was just too much for the Indian women, since it was so rare for any outsider to speak their language, but to have a stranger walk up with strange, big objects on straps around his chest and shout, "I've got to take a piss," sent them into gales of laughter. The photographer stayed perplexed the whole time he was there. We never told him what he was saying.

I think that if I ever win the lottery, I'll go back to Dourados and work with the Guarani.

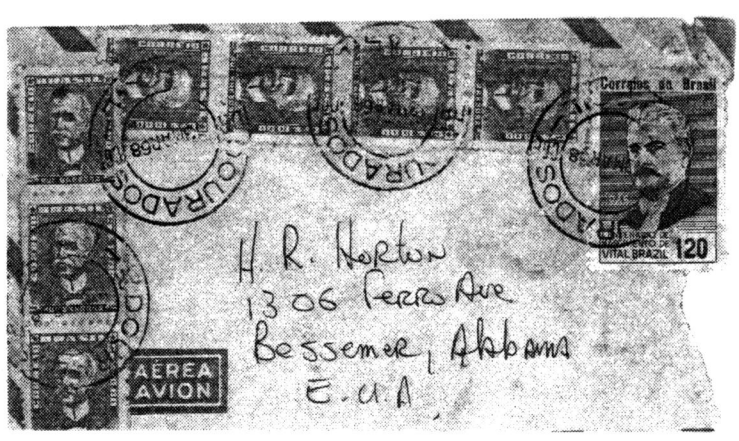

Hi Folks,

Peace Corps Syndrome

Long time since I've written. Things are happening, like cold. It's real cold here, particularly when there are no heaters, hot water, or well made houses. Getting along beautifully at the Post. I like the people and they like me. I'm getting on a garden for the orphanage here, also buying materials and having the kids here in the vila make two toys; they keep one and give one to an orphan. Did I tell you about my 5 guinea pigs? One couple (she's expecting) and one mother with two young ones. I'm making a 9-10 foot bed with built-in bookshelves.

You can send my mail to Caixa Postal 321, Dourados. It looks like I'm staying. The parrot sends you his love. No word from Ann, Clara, or anyone lately; guess due to my poor correspondence. We showed movies last week here on an outside wall (sheet) and had about 50 people. Showed four, the rest (films) were backwards, upside down, so I'm saving them. Don't know how the cold will affect my garden.

I'm at Janice's; we're using the lamps for heat more than light. Still no lights in the apartment, and no water for about a week. It's hard keeping clean and then when you do have it, it's too cold to bathe. The best time is mid-day in the sun (enclosed backyard). There's been a mob of people passing through here in the last few days, four volunteers, a missionary.

I guess I've written myself dry. Love to all. Sure am glad I packed my woolens. I'm going to Fatima next week to get the rest of my things and close the apartment. I won't be back there. It's amazing how you have to change lines of thinking and reasoning in the P.C.

Ate logo,
Ron

Ron Horton

INDIAN TRIBES

In the mid 1960's, I was pretty unaware of the Amazon Indian tribes except from the demented minds of Hollywood and still in awe of the religious adventurers called missionaries. When I got to drive a Jeep from Campo Grande to Cuiaba, several months after I arrived, I bumped into a Peace Corps Volunteer from the far north of the state, up toward the wilder parts just south of the Amazon Basin. Mark set it up for me to meet the widows of the two missionaries killed by a tribe after they flew in for the very first contact with outsiders; their story made famous by an article in Readers Digest in 1965. The two widowed wives were just flying back into the same river landing where their husbands had been killed the year before. I got to meet them over shortwave just before they touched down, At the time I was impressed by them, not yet realizing just how insane these zealots were, determined to give them Jesus, and the ruination brought on by contact when the Indians were already living with God, as they had done for thousands of years. Yet, these missionaries thought their way was better.

Our local Indians were the Guarani Kaiowa, Xavante, Camba, the Guato and the Kaidweu. Mark and several of the other far northern Mato Grossan PCV'S had done quite a bit of trade, thinking they were helping the Indians by buying and selling such things as beautiful strings of hishi bead necklaces, actual bows and arrows, game clubs, macramé hammocks and such. As broke as I was, I spent every dime that I had on such items, like two sets of ceremonial bows given to young men when they killed their first jaguar, every inch of the bows covered in red or blue feathers, the game clubs they used to finish the tapir or deer they usually only wounded with the arrows, having to chase the critter for miles until bashing it with these purple wooded four-foot devices as beautifully balanced and made as any Samurai sword. The one I bought was appreciated by my friends for five or six years before it was stolen. I am still so attached to the beauty of that game club that 20 years after its theft I still think of somehow magically winning the lottery and being able to advertise some outlandish reward for its return.

The arrows ranged from fishing points made with black barbs lashed onto rounded hardwood shafts inset into bamboo main stems with split flight feather veins glued and lashed onto the ends; blunt ended arrows for stunning the macaws they took to raise for a permanent supply of feathers; and the broad heads made by splitting off an eight inch section out of the side of a rounded hardwood stock. Most of the crafts were from the Nambuquari and Bororro tribes north of Cuiaba'; their crafts painted a delightful picture of these peoples. I tried to play the little four-inch nose flutes, two rounded sections of a gourd glued with sap, one hole for one nostril's breath and two other small holes to make music. I couldn't afford the exquisite macramé hammocks and feather garments.

Then 1000 miles to the south, I met the Guarani who had been contacted and SAVED only a few years before, seemingly without crafts, living in squalor, full of TB and VD, and though I didn't realize it at the time, only a small percentage of them had survived the smallpox and measles that had raped their civilization.

Though many Brazilians had Indian, black and Portuguese blood, there was still a lot of prejudice against the Indians and the real dark blacks. There was something like 20 words to describe just how black a person was. I was so naively green in 1966 that I never realized that prejudice until 20 years later. That's pretty damned naïve, but that was how I was then. Unfortunately, I didn't have

Ron Horton

the sense to spend time with their medicine men and learn some of the thousands of years of botanical pharmaceutical knowledge by studing their plants.

7/6/67

Hi Folks,
I'm still in the process of building my bed, bookshelves, clothes thing, and hope to get on a bar for the kitchen soon. A mob of P.C.V.'s have been through... Vivian three times, she's on her way home, the girl in Vila Gloria is changing to here; she'll probably live with Janice. Bought a blanket today; it's cold here. I was sick yesterday, fever of 101, but it's gone. I'm a little weak and sore, probably a cold or flu coming on. The Syrians I eat with are really grim about the war. I hope the cease fire succeeds though I believe W.W.III is on soon. I think things will be jumping (changing) here soon (with the P.C.) vamose ver (we'll see). Still no water here. We're heating it when we can find it, to sponge bathe. Expecting a small raise in July, all prices have gone up since Christmas. I'm still planning on the Amazon or close to in about 30 days. Any news from Clara, Jack, Ann, or Bill? Summer vacation already. Bye for now.
Ron

19 de Junho, 1967

Alo A minha familia,

I've written several letters but keep forgetting to mail them. I've got one to go with this tomorrow. The house, bed, etc., is beginning to shape up. I'm writing on my table for the first time in months, brought it up from Fatima about two weeks ago. I think I mentioned this in my other letter. Got one drawer in the bed. Still one bookcase to go, plus a

Peace Corps Syndrome

breakfast bar for the kitchen.

Went to a fazenda this weekend, Oh I told you that I think; my mind's slipping. I'm ready to begin painting. Got a letter from Ann telling me I'm to receive a sweater. How wonderful with this cold weather. Today wasn't cold, 78 degrees, beautiful. Started the garden today, have to turn the earth, fence it, put manure and fertilizer in, seed beds. I'm putting in carrots, lettuce, onions, cabbage, couve, beets, radishes, water melons, cantaloupes, pole beans, some white beans, okra, etc. Hope to teach some of the kids how to garden (as soon as I learn). Glad the map got through.

I'm growing a mustache again. Nothing else to do. Work is going well. Plan to vacation the 1st of July. Heard you went to Jacks from Ann. Must go. Love.
Ron

28 de Junho, 67

Hi,
Well, I start vacation in a week. Still don't know where to go, and it won't be far with the money I have. Think I'm going camping somewhere close by here in the South.

Looks as if I'll be the head lab tech beginning when I get back from my 18 days. Things are going well, the garden is just about going. Oh, your Christmas gifts, two turtlenecks arrived, thanks, I love them. They'll be great down here. I have one more package coming, hope Ann's gift is coming through.

Janice just got back from C.G., and I don't have to take the rabies series again. We've had two cats and 3 rabbits to die. Hummph. I have a pistol (snake protection), now I need a 22 to down small game: birds, alligators (for preservation). I'm getting organized for the trip, making snake bags. I have to get my hammock, make some traps, re-learn how to snake, etc. Home by now seems 1000000 miles and 100 years ago. I'd really love to get there. I'm trying to get something off for Rhonda. Got a letter two or three months ago. Are you all back from vacation yet, alive and well. Thanks again for the turtlenecks. I'm off to eat soon and to bring Janice's supper back. What happened to the H.O.B.I.B.D.P. (Help Our Boy in Brazil Dollar Program)? Caught a new snake, have him in a cage; bought a big turtle, about 18 inches long, the same type as the gopher turtle we have in South Alabama. We now have a turtle, an owl, a snake, and one parrot. I hope after my trip we'll have more. Well, I must be off.*

Love,
Ron
My mustache is growing again.

BRAZILIAN BUGS

You may think you've seen bugs, but not until you go to Brazil and are forced to sleep under mosquito nets where only 10 or 15 B-29s inside with you is a blessing. The sound of mosquitoes in one house I lived in was so loud, I remember telling myself one night when I came in late to my screenless abode, without electricity, running water, or bathroom that the mosquito drone was equal to being in an airport with planes taking off. Flying rhinoceros beetles were so obscenely huge that one knocked off and broke the 18-inch tall glass on my Aladdin kerosene lamp. Butterflies were like psychedelic clouds on riverbanks, particularly in the dry season when the water splashed onto the river bank by trucks and buses would attract tens or hundreds of thousands. Their huge squadrons of color shifts, since many were different colors on upstroke and down stroke, were like iridescent giants that flew through the canopy of the jungle in strobe light action as they first blazed in magnificence blue iridescence and then disappeared until the next wing beat. Sometimes the river banks had mixed colors, but often shoals of a dozen varieties in distinct color zones would just overwhelm me. Before I left the States, I had written the Smithsonian Institute and had gotten a free insect collecting kit replete with hundreds of long thin pins and mounts to affix wings and such. Soon I had hundreds of different colored, unusually iridescent beetles and butterflies, a true Smithsonian level natural treasure until other bugs ate my bugs; I never had a glass cover.

My more memorable insect moments were with ants. Every day one would see thousands of really huge leaf cutters taking trees for a walk, thousands of 8 to12 foot tall termite mounds on every bus trip, and army ants were not uncommon. Almost all of these just mentioned species had larger warrior or guard members with mandibles a good quarter of an inch across. People in the bush, either Indians or the poor, would use these big guys, particularly the leaf cutter guards since they were so available, to suture a cut. All you had to do was to grab one behind the head and hold his head across the cut, letting him bite each side of the cut with those grotesquely huge mandibles and twist off the head while genetics kept him biting the enemy attacking his column.

My first ant adventure came when I took my mid service two week vacation. I had planned for over a year to finally get up north to the Amazon and my friends from training on a boat trip, but I was so broke that all I could afford was to go into Campo Grande and hang out with Doctor Bill awhile and go camping in the jungle. I had a hammock, some wire for a trip wire around my camp, a double barreled 22 calibre Derringer, and by god, I was going to camp out in the jungle by myself. I was going to conquer my fears of being alone in the jungle at night. So, late one afternoon Bill drove me about 15 miles out until the jungle got thick; I grabbed my gear and walked off as Bill asked after me, "Are you sure about this?" When I turned back and grimly nodded, taking a deep breath, he said, "Okay, see you tomorrow," before he sped off back to civilization. My camp was on a little knoll about 100 yards from the dirt trail the jeep had crept through. I set up my hammock, put my trip wire about a foot off the ground all the way around me, and hung my food about six feet off the ground in a tree. Then I gathered some squaw wood and built a small fire. Lying back in my hammock, I once again experienced the thrill of Brazil's interior star show and jungle sounds alone, no lights as my fire burned out, eleven gigabytes of stars illuminating the mosquitoes and other night flying blood suckers now swarming over any uncovered area of my tender flesh or crawling down any opening to gnaw away at their heart's content. Finally, I dropped off, thank god.

Bill was so curious to see if I was alive that he arrived about nine thirty, early for him, and we drove off to Campo Grande, first to the fried fish place for brunch and beer, then over to a sidewalk café to sip a few caipiriras, the country club for an afternoon swim, and back to Bill's back yard on the patio under the grape arbor to chill for a while. Just before dark we packed up and went to the Figueira restaurant for dinner. Bill had decided that he was going to camp out with me since I was still alive after the first night, no jaguar bites being obvious.

So out into dark night we drove again, down the little trail into the jungle to my camp. Using a small weak flashlight, I walked toward the high ground of my camp. As I shone the light around, something caught my eye on the food cache. My god, giant ants the size of cocker

Peace Corps Syndrome

spaniels had cut open all my food packages, entire crackers were magically being taken down the tree to the ants' home. My campsite, the knoll, was a gigantic ant mound the size of twenty 1950 Buick station wagons. Bill ran screaming like a girl. I had just enough presence to cut my hammock down before I caught up with the moving jeep.

My second ant experience was many times more exciting since it required me to fight army ants with torches when I was pretty damned drunk in order to save my rabbit hutches. The second time I tried to afford living at the apartment complex where Janice lived (she always had a little extra money from her savings from nursing), I had so many pets it was like a zoo: Monkeys, parrots, ducks, turtles, a nine-foot anaconda and two rabbit cages on the backyard patio. These apartments had an outdoor tiled floor patio, six-foot walls with broken glass shards as defense against anyone trying to come over, and a toilet and shower in a roofed back corner.

I had my rabbit hutches along the back wall of the patio. One evening coming home from drinking or whoring, the electricity was off, of course, when I walked in the door. I remember staggering out to the toilet and while reeling back into the house, I noticed the wall looked fuzzier than normal in the moonlight. Somehow, I made it back inside and lay down and tried to keep my swirling head on the pillow, but I was troubled by the fuzzy wall image. Finally, I got up and walked back to the patio wall. I lit a match and screamed, "Oh my god!" A three-foot wide section of the wall was blanketed with millions of giant army ants coming over the wall and up the legs of my rabbit hutches.

The rabbits were panicking in their boxes and were running in and out. The kerosene that I kept in the small cans I had set each leg of the two cages into had gone dry, had evaporated, and the ants were after my rabbits. The rabbits were still alive since it was hard for the ants to make it across the wire bottoms. I grabbed some paper and wadding it into a twist, lit it and began to fight the army ants. I had to burn almost every book I had. There were thousands and thousands of the ants, inches thick in their attack swarm, and I was really drunk, but finally they stopped coming over the wall just as I gave out of paper and matches.

Aug 9, 1967

Hi,
Just got letters from you and Rhonda. Was that the first time you've flown? Things are hectic here at the moment. I've taken over in the Lab, and am trying to encourage something opposite to ignorance in the assistants. I moved again (only a few feet) to two rooms and close to the city water system. I'm going to improvise with some hose pipe for a shower. I've started drawing a little, still hope to get an art class started here. Have five or six people interested in lessons……

My new house is still dusty, though newer and therefore easier to keep clean. Mosquitoes are terrible; repellent doesn't seem to do the job entirely, so I guess I'll have to put up a mosquito net. I hope you got my letter telling you not to send anything else down. The only things I can think of that I need are my brushes in my room and a few tubes of paint.

I'm sending some Brazilian currency to you to keep for me, or frame or whatever you want to do with it. I guess you heard the ex-President (two months) was killed in a plane crash. No one here seemed to be bothered; he wasn't very popular. I'm including some negatives, will send more in each letter. I'm off to clean house and clean up.
Love to all. Ron

Peace Corps Syndrome

12 de Agosto, 1967

Hi,
Haven't received any mail all this week. Got you a big letter off today; I wrote five days ago. A quiet week. Unexpectedly received 45 mil in the Bank yesterday. Maybe it's our raise. It sure was nice. Preserved several turtles and frogs today. Think I'll keep my big turtule as a pet. I've been painting my doors and windows. I decided to brighten up the neighborhood. Going to paint the house in shades of blue. I'm at a Brazilian house at the moment, talking and helping her clean. She's very sweet, knows a few words in English, very intelligent, quite cute, very young. Her father gives me Scotch. I think we are going to a party tonight (in the rain) at the social club. She's a doll. Very nice to have a young thing around to cheer up an old codger like me. Put in a shower yesterday, i.e. shower head and hose pipe from the neighborhood faucet. I'm being unusually productive....
Love,
Ron

Ron Horton

PEACE CORPS AND THE CIA

When I arrived in Brazil in 1966 the country had just been taken over by a military junta, however the USA relationship stayed the same between the two countries. Machine gun packing soldiers were everywhere, airports, borders, around any big governmental buildings; state capitals like Cuiaba' had four teams of rather poor looking Tommy-gun wielding, pants too short soldiers around the governor's walled compounds. Brazilians, with virtually every natural resource on earth had an attitude of impending national greatness and any meddling by the USA was a constant issue in the tabloids.

When two American geology students touring northern Brazil collected some rocks and minerals, they were arrested and made national headlines for weeks on end. **"USA Meddling Thieves Trying to Steal Brazil's Mineral Wealth"** were the actual headlines. Being 23-24 years old and naively green, I was unprepared for what happened next. The Peace Corps office in Rio was bombed! I had just been there a few months before. No Americans were injured, but a Brazilian national office worker lost a hand.

On moving to Dourados in 1967, I chanced upon an outdoor restaurant a few blocks from the Health Post where I worked each morning. There were two neat immigrant Arabs who had built the place, the Brazilian frontier was full of Japanese, Germans, Arabs and others... little ethnic walk-in cafes all over Brazil. For eight to twelve bucks, I could buy lunch for a month. The owners and I became friends as time went by; the meals were unique to me, falafel, tripe, tongue, great Syrian-Lebanese cuisine and soon I was having a caipiringa (a double shot of 100 proof cachaxa with a whole lime and about two tablespoons of sugar) which cost all of 100 cruzeiros (about three cents

Peace Corps Syndrome

American). The first couple of weeks I was there, flies would inevitably land and find their way into my drink, as I indulged in what grew to be one of my favorite pastimes, sitting in a sidewalk café and watching life go by. Early on, I would throw the fly infested drink away, but after watching the local custom, I soon began to dip out drunk or drowned flies with a casual flip of my finger. Otherwise, you'd never get to finish the sugar and lime, brain numbing tumbler of corn liquor.

The restaurant owners always had on radio Cairo while I had lunch, and I became accustomed to this rare music that wasn't Brazilian samba. On days when there was nothing going on with a community development project, I would often spend an hour and a half or two hours over lunch, writing letters, sipping, watching donkey taxis go by from the bus station. I rarely ate there at night, but on one occasion I was at the restaurant one night by myself. I had just paid my check, stepping down the two steps from the inside of the restaurant onto the wide outdoor veranda on the corner of a main street with lots of people around when a Brazilian doctor I recognized walked up to me, blocking my way and began to scream. "You fucking CIA, god damned Americans messing around with our country, you S.O.B."

The guy was bobbing and almost frothing at the mouth in front of me. I took his pusillanimous umbrage with great insult and got in his face. "You're wrong, no damn way," I shouted. "Sou voluntario da paz, sozinho!" Finally I had to step around him while he kept on screaming, "You fucking CIA." I was so unaware of how much the US and the CIA were involved and had been with all the military dictatorships, drug cartels, and banana republics. Just meddling, as when Henry Kissinger was responsible for the assassination of the democratically elected but communist president of Chile, President Allende.

In 1967, Peace Corps had me drive an old Jeep 600

miles up the Pan-American highway to Cuiaba' where I met a Time magazine reporter who interviewed me and several other PCV'S for an article he was working on just days before the Arab-Israeli War of 67 broke out. He dropped by to see me just before he left for the Middle East to cover the fighting saying that he would be back to finish our story. I later read about his death in the magazine. He was killed a few days after he arrived in the war zone.

After flying back to Campo Grande and busing six hours back to Dourados, I dropped by the Arab restaurant the next day. Radio Cairo was blaring that US planes off carriers had attacked cities in Egypt and Syria; suddenly, my Syrian and Lebanese friends were in my face screaming at me, only this time it hurt more as they screamed hatred at me. "You fucking Americans." So I lost my favorite hangout and noon meal deal.

I thought they were absolutely crazy until sometime in the late 1980's while I was in graduate school, I found a very small article on a back page of the *Northwest Arkansas Times* about a senate investigative committee that had solicited testimony that U.S. Navy planes had indeed attacked targets in both Syria and Egypt in 1967; the U.S. jets fighting alongside Israel. Also, while I was in graduate school in Fayetteville, Arkansas (87-94), the George Bush-CIA cocaine scandal broke, and I stood five feet from the freelance CIA pilot who had been flying C-130's to Columbia carrying guns to the Contras and flying big mysterious bundles back to Mena, Arkansas. He told us that he always reported to George Bush's #1 liaison man upon his return, and when he finally opened one of the bundles they always bought back to the States and discovered it was cocaine and reported that to Bush's man, the SOB said, "So what, shut up about it and mind your own damned business". Apparently the pilot thought that it was his business and had just gone public with his story. He made one of his first public appearances at Fayetteville

Peace Corps Syndrome

before testifying before Congress. One of the other pilots on those missions died a very mysterious death... go figure.

In the 1960's, just like the Bush brats in the 1990's in Texas and Florida, the Rockefellers had their daddy buy them governorships. Winthrop had established his domain in Arkansas, and as it turned out was a 40% owner of a 500,000 hectares (over one million acre) ranch in Brazil. The ranch made up a very large chunk of western Mato Grosso, over 120 kilometers wide. Foreigners couldn't own land outright, so the Arkansas governor had become partners with the finance minister of Brazil. A friend of mine, Al _____, was dating the daughter of the ranch's manager who owned the other 20% of the ranch, and asked me and a beautiful Peace Corps Volunteer I had hardly been around to go with him for a visit. I forget her name, but she and I took the single car tram ride west from Campo Grande to join Al who was already there. The ranch was fabulous, a serious cattle train depot where they marketed over 50,000 head of cattle a year. Ranch hands met us and drove us to the main hacienda, the largest ranch house in the world it seemed, with long multiple wings of rooms with windows on two or three sides. My room was plush, like a suite with private bath, mosquito nets over the bed just like back home, gorgeous ranch made chairs and tables in the exotic colors of jungle hardwoods. Outside were gorgeous tropical shrubs and fruit trees, more wildlife than I had yet seen.

It took me a couple of days to make friends with the 10-12 boxers that had the run of the grounds and seemed to be playing with each other most of the time. At the largest round wooden dinner table I'd ever seen, about 12-14 of us ate some of the finest food I have eaten in my life: Al, the ranch manager, Mona, his beautiful daughter whom Al was dating, a pilot, two foremen, and so on. My very first finger bowls puzzled me for several minutes until others showed me the way. I remember one could drop an ash in an ashtray, turn to talk, and magically the ashes would be gone. There were dozens of servants, probably hundreds of cowboys for this million acre ranch.

Being a biology nut, I dug around a dried up waterway, it being the dry season, and magically dug up a South American lungfish in its mucous plug in the only damp spot left under a big rock in the very lowest spot, though at the time I had no idea on earth what it was. I found some bright colored tree frogs in the house's water tank and generally had a good time.

The ranch was so large that they had their own tannery, the size of a basketball arena with dozens of concrete vats where skins soaked. I bought two pair of over the knee skin-tight chaps that looked like pirate boots without the bottoms. The cowboys would put them on before putting on the classic Brazilian floppy, wide at the top, henna red boots. This was serious thorn country when on horseback, and some cowboys had entire outfits of stiff leather even to little leather helmets. I hung around the cowboys as they loaded Brahma and zebu cattle fresh off the range into railroad cattle cars. They first drove them into a 12-foot high solid timber pen. Miraculously, one steer, jumping and using his slaughterhouse bound comrades as stepping stones, cleared the barricade and tore off, followed by five or six cowboys yelling almost in glee, flailing their stiff rawhide lariats only when they got within a few feet. No Hollywood here, just real short over the head tosses.

The week ended in being invited to go fishing with the owner-manager on Sunday (Sunday was the only day when fishing was allowed on the ranch). We drove north past the rail line into extremely thick jungle to a riverbank where enormous, 30 foot, dugout wooden canoes with big outboard motors awaited us. I sat in the middle of the giant, hand hollowed, sculpted boat as we whizzed up river past screaming howler monkeys; the first time I had seen them. A big bunch of them, howling like banshees,

Peace Corps Syndrome

drowned out the outboard noise. When we stopped to fish, Giorgio handed me an 18 foot cane pole, a lot like the ones I used growing up in Alabama, but thicker. Rather than 6 lb. Test, these had what looked like the 300 lb. line they used as leader on red snapper boats out of Panama City, Florida. And the line was tied all the way down the length of the pole and on to the floor where a big coil of it lay; the end tied off to a gunwale. "If the fish is too big to handle, just throw the pole over" Giorgio grinned.

The common fish I had seen all over Mato Grosso were 40-60 pound Pacu shaped like a piranha (imagine a forty pound bluegill bream and big green catfish with big black spots called pintados that were all seemingly 5 to 6 feet), so I knew he wasn't kidding. I soon discovered there were three species of piranha as some of the most beautiful red, green, and gold 12 to18-inch toothy varmints soon covered the area around the other two guys in the boat. They caught a lot more fish that I did and obviously had more experience taking the hooks out of the man eaters. One catch was a 25 pound catfish, so transparent you could see through its head. Macaws swooping across the river, toucans in the underside of the treetops munching down on fruit, schools of piranha coming through the colored water, obviously in swarms since nobody would catch fish for a while, and Wham, then everyone would have man eating varmints on the line. Extremely good tasting fish.

When the time came for me to get back to Dourados, the owner offered to fly me back to Campo Grande on one of the ranch's two, single-engine Cessna's. As I walked up to the planes for the first time, I saw the stickers "Donated by U.S.A. Foreign Aid" on both planes. Suddenly, I wished I had looked more closely at the two monster bulldozers they had pointed out, saying they were the absolute largest in the world. They were capable of clearing acres and acres of jungle a day to create more pasture.

I loaded my gear, and we took off at mid-day heading

east to Campo Grande, several hours of flight time ahead. There were a few cumulus clouds as we took off; miles to the east was a small mountain range we could see in the distance, but just as we began to gain altitude as the hills jumped up, the ceiling fell out. You couldn't see 100-feet in front of the plane. The damned pilot kept on, and I swear we felt our way up the hillside with my stomach dragging the ground. We finally made it over the hills and just as we leveled out we had no visibility at all. Then without a word, inexplicably, the pilot turned and flew back into the mountain range. No instruments, no visible anything until it was 50 feet in front of us. Once again we crept up the mountains and all the way back to the ranch. I caught the next train out the following morning. Damn U.S. Aid donated plane, about as good as the warehouse of U.S. Aid, water spoiled, bulgur wheat in Cuiaba', or the other big shipment of food aid that was doled out by some priests only when money changed hands.

24 de Agosto, 67

Mail has been scarce lately, received one or two from you. How is the day shift working out? Does he like it?

Things are blah here. I'm back in the blah situation I was in while in Fatima de Sul. Thank God it's only two weeks till conference. We'll be leaving the sixth, I think.

If it wasn't for the two year deal, I'd be home now. I'm going to talk to the boss at conference, maybe go to Santo Antonio do Leveger (I was there a week my first month in Brazil) or get my walking papers.

When the other lab tech left, I began to initiate some changes (better techniques); some have caught on, but I guess I was too fast or too pushy, because there's a

Peace Corps Syndrome

rebellion in our midst. Just small things, but to show that the American can see where to get off. It's a shame we're still regarded as strangers, only passers through. I've decided Peace Corps should only be involved in teaching, otherwise, it's a waste of time and effort.

Almost no service today in the lab as it's chilly, cloudy, and was drizzly. The people never come on days like this. It was unbearably hot three days ago, much dust and the people are saying it's going to be a long hot summer. I just hate to come home empty handed, with nothing to show for this year. If I come now, I have to pay my way home, and it would take all that's accumulated. I'm still in the thought process. Will let you know as it develops. Much love. Get Dad to carry you dancing.
Ron

Vitor and Lydia

The apartment complex called Vila Dreyfus, where Janice lived in Dourados on the western outskirts of town, was just to the dusty right of a corner store saloon. There always seemed to be two or three horses tied up out front and a crew drinking shots at a crude wooden bar, next to giant coils of tobacco one-inch wide, rows of huge salted fish stacked like half sheets of white sheetrock, and big burlap bags of rice and black beans closest to the door. Just beyond the dagger wearing, pistol toting cowboys was the apartment complex, the exact same reddish brown color of the mud during the six month rainy season and the dust during the six month dry season. The rows of apartments were built of simple plaster, long straight facades with doors only in the front every 16 to18 feet. Most of the doors were usually open, with someone leaning halfway out.

I was living two doors down from Janice in my second year in Brazil when a cute couple close to Janice's age moved in across the street from her. Vitor had a VW van with double wide doors, called a Kombi, which he used to run a bus line from Dourados to Maracaju, about three hours away by mud or dust roads. Lydia was a sweet, big-chested girl, and we all became friends pretty danged fast. It wasn't long before they asked me and Janice to go with them on weekend trips. Vitor was always so gracious on his bus line to the 12 to16 people he seemed to be able to pack into the VW, along with that many giant burlap bags of rice or beans, not to mention the chickens in cages on top. He went out of his way helping his passengers' lives be a little better and nicer. As a result, he became a very popular person; he and Lydia were fought over to be the weekend guests of different folks out on their ranches or farms; frontier people always seemed to be so unbelievably open in welcoming guests into their homes.

When I say out in the country, you really have no idea, but you do need to know that the main roads were muddy quagmires, impassable you'd think by anything less than a bulldozer; bridges had to be literally rebuilt after every vehicle crossed. Most of the places we visited were off this great turnpike of commerce... another 10 to 40 miles on really bad excuses for roads...so far, in fact, that no electric lights were within a hundred miles at least. The trick with the VW, which Vitor liked for me to drive when I went with him on his bus route so he could flirt with the ladies, was to mash the gas pedal to the floorboard and NEVER let up until you had to stop at the next town or slow down for cattle drives.

One family that Vitor took us to visit consisted of a 45-year-old father and mother and three strong sons, all recently married to apparently very fertile, good looking women. I don't know how many hundreds of acres they had at the family farm they had settled about ten years before, but it was a large homestead, and they had leased an additional 500 hectares of prime bottom land just where the bus route crossed a small river. Loide and his sons had dug six-feet-deep drainage ditches for what looked liked miles to control the water so they could grow rice, and they had just bought a giant, two-wheeled cultivator for their perfect, rice growing farm.

Once visiting out at the rice project with Vitor, I met Loide's four field hands who lived in a 16 by 12 foot, thatch covered, stick and mud shed and worked from first light to last, for two meals a day and one thousand Brazilian dollars (about 40 cents). Loide grinned real big as we all squatted down and said, "Ronaldo, these two guys are both escaped murderers," and these two good natured young men, right beside me, told me about escaping from a jail, one in Sao Paulo, the other from way up north in Minas Gerais.. I wasn't really that upset at the idea of socializing with criminals, having gotten over that kind of shock a few months before. A rancher I had met from Maracaju, a big local hotshot, had gotten a little upset when federal police pulled over his young son for not having the ownership papers for his father's jeep and then held him in jail for several hours. Well, the rancher obviously thought he had right on his side when he immediately drove into town on learning of his son's suffering, murdered the federal officer on the spot with a pistol, in broad daylight in front of everybody, turned around and drove home, and NO one ever came out to even talk to or chide him. That was Brazil. Once, Janice sent one of the darling little girls that hung around like little puppies to the store just at dusk, and after just a minute or so she came screaming back into the apartment. "Meu deus, meu deus" was all that she could say for a long time. Finally, we learned that one of our casual friends from the neighborhood had shot and killed some cowboy just as our little friend walked in.

Ron Horton

These weekend visits out into the varjao (bush) were excuses for all day visiting and playing around the farms or fazendas of our soon to be dear friends, idyllic spots that had been carved out of thick jungle by burning and slashing. Macaws and toucans were everywhere in the tree tops, anteaters and emus in the beginnings of the savannah openings. Once Vitor stopped for me when we approached one adult Emu with seemingly dozens of babies following behind; I felt only a little ridiculous as I actually chased them, just like Wiley Coyote, watching them disappear into the bush. Sometimes I'd chase the flocks of tens of thousands of wild doves around with an exotic 28 gauge double-barreled shotgun, almost like a little toy. Sometimes we'd have sharp-shooting contests with different guns, 38 calibre pistolas or derringers like the one I had for a short while when I decided to go campout in the jungle by myself. The 22 calibre Derringers kicked like a mule and hitting a barn was considered a miracle.

Mainly, we'd just hang around, enjoying the typical goings on of life on the frontier. When meals were being prepared, the cook would sometimes fix long, sword like skewers for each person; you'd cut off the outside strips of meat as they seared in the fire, putting the skewer back on throughout the feast, but usually the meat was sun-dried jerky. The 28 gauge had been loaned to me by a wealthy rancher who was also trying to help me connect with Mom in Alabama by way of his ham radio. Mom had gotten worried about me in the middle of 1968 when I really began to freak out and hadn't written home in several months. This was after Janice had returned to the States, the draft was looming up on the horizon, and once again Peace Corps had screwed me around by forgetting to pay me for months on end. The main office in Rio had been blown up a few months back, and several different state directors had moved on or come on board. It was often very disorganized for us volunteers in the field.

Peace Corps Syndrome

I was bitter and disillusioned, and found it increasingly difficult to carry on; I was more than ready to go home. First, they had kidnapped me from the Amazon and sent me where I didn't have a real job, where I was not needed, and without warm clothes in the chilly winters of southern Mato Grosso. Then when Janice and I created the traveling health clinic for the Indians, a new director came along and demanded we stop doing the work and giving the inoculations to the Indians. It all seemed so insane and banal; I was really kind of beside myself. By this time when they told me to return to a totally redundant, useless half day at the Health Post doing nothing, I told the new kid director to go bury his head in his ass.

For the last four or five months I was in Brazil I became a rebel; I just didn't give a damn. I had read some stuff about agricultural output falling behind the exponential population growth rate in Brazil and was suddenly horribly aware that every person I helped survive would be the parent of six to eight kids, and grandparents to many more in 20 years, and every year there would be less food, more distended stomachs from Kwashikora, fewer Indians. I had changed from being a gung-ho volunteer to a washed out, spent, prostitute of a young American. A battle fatigued, empty face stared out at me from the mirror.

I actually did go back to the Health Post for a while. A dear little Brazilian colleague at the lab had gone to Cuiaba for a year for lab-tech training, had returned to the Post and was doing a really great job as the new director. Natalia had two assistant lab-techs, and I literally was in the way. I respected the new director too much to get in the way, now that they had a good, functioning lab. The Indians were still dying and not being treated, but the bureaucrats insisted they knew best. I was starting to get an attitude, and would have become even more bitter and disillusioned, but for the fantastic good-naturedness of Vitor and Lydia and the families we visited...sweet people, largely without excess ego or so called civilization.

Loide quickly learned he could razzle-dazzle me with snake tales since I was so crazy about reptiles. A few months before I had asked several of Vitor's bus patrons to keep an eye out for snakes for my rapidly developing zoo. One caught a nine-foot anaconda, so I went with Vitor out to Loide's to pick up my snake. When I opened the box, this beautiful dark green snake with black spots the size of silver dollars poked his head around and out, a head about the size of my two hands together on top of each other. I thought that I'd get his attention with my right hand and grab for his head with my left. The snake was faster and chomped down on my left hand, his ½ to ¾ -inch teeth hit bone, blood flying everywhere. Loide and his three sons, the two escaped murderers, and Vitor were all behind me until the anaconda bit me; they all ran screaming like women while I grabbed it and put it down in the sack.

To them I was a "Hombre," young and green maybe, but they all seemed to dote on me, kidding me and just being tremendously nice. Loide's rice fields stretched from the muddy road off into the distance, and on a regular basis long "S" shaped curves could be seen snaking off into the paddies. "Anaconda" Vitor tweaked as he grinned past the 17-year-old, nubile beauty rubbing against him on the front seat of the Kombe as we passed Loide's fields one day. I had the occasion when visiting to follow these tracks for what seemed like miles. Sometime they seemed to be wide enough to accommodate some damned big heavy animals, the way the rice was flattened and pushed out, as if a ten thousand pound basketball or medicine bag had been rolled sensuously to the horizon.

Loide and the crew harvested all the rice with small hand scythes. One day we were trapped under the veranda during a rainy season deluge; he was grinning that great smile through three missing teeth and trying to make me believe that a cow vertebre he had brought in was from a

Peace Corps Syndrome

snake. He told me about chopping rice stalks the year before when a big 22-24 foot anaconda he hadn't seen struck at his hand just as he swung his short handled scythe, and how he had hacked the snake's head off and cooked the snake down for its oil. He never did say how he used the oil.

Seu Loide, Vitor and all of them thought I was telling tales one day when I mentioned a can opener. Canned food was so rarely seen that on several occasions different groups of Brazilian friends would ask to hear the "tale of the mythical can opener," and they would laugh till they dropped, thinking I was lying to make them laugh…a machine to open cans…ha ha ha…

To this day I remember Loide and family as some of the dearest, sweetest people I have ever met. I can still clearly see their beautiful spread of houses and fields, a twenty acre clearing among the green towering trees on the edges of the jungle. Some of the trees looked out of place; they were so unbelievably tall they stretched up and up, having grown tall and spindly only because they had matured over the centuries amidst the most exotic hardwoods I have ever seen. Some of the wood was deep purple while others were a deep orange.

The evenings always began with crepuscular, calcophanized flights of dozens of parrots and toucans into the surrounding jungle. Little conical homemade tin lamps, like coal miner's lights, warmed the dirt floored houses into an oasis from what seemed like wild savagery just a few feet away. Judging from the number of insects that flew into the light, we were damned lucky we didn't have anything stronger to attract them, or we would have certainly been eaten alive.

After breakfast in the mornings I would often take my borrowed double-barreled 28 gauge, a delightful little gun, and go off adventuring. Sometimes hundreds of small green parrots would fly out of the fields when Loide, or one of his sons, would blast away trying to save the corn which they grew mainly for food for the livestock. I never shot anything but two of the wild doves that wisped up from the fields in the thousands. Birds occurred in such numbers in the jungle that at times they resembled smoke or blowing clouds. Loide looked and talked at me, long and hard, to make sure I understood exactly where the trip-wired, old single-barrel shot gun set one foot above the ground was located, set to kill the wild pigs raiding their gardens back toward a creek side of the property. I spotted the trip wire, thank god, and went down to the river hoping I would see a tapir, but I never had the good fortune. The giant anteater out at the ranch's entrance was definitely the most exotic animal I ever saw. What a beautiful name in Portuguese, Tamandua Bandeira. I'm ashamed to say that I actually bought a skin of one just before I left Mato Grosso in 1968.

Loide had an old swayback, worn out, white horse that he and Vitor decided I needed, rather than the Peace Corps bicycle that I rarely used. The mud in the rainy season was impassible and during the dry season you couldn't see three feet through the giant rolling clouds of dust that blotted out the smog from millions of acres of burning brush and forests; the buses ignored the no visibility and roared out of this blur at 40 mph. Anyhow, I found myself going with Vitor toward Loide's, my bicycle on top of the Kombi to be traded for the old white horse, the plan being that I would start back the next morning for the thirty-five mile horseback ride to Dourados.

After coffee and mamao the next morning, Loide began to demonstrate the uniquely Brazilian manner of saddling a horse. First was a blanket, then a saddle without the girth attached. The girth went completely around the horse and saddle, above the seat, and then a thick sheepskin was placed on top with another complete girth strap to be cinched up. Of course the stirrups were about a foot too short for me at their maximum expansion. So about nine

Peace Corps Syndrome

o'clock I set out to ride the one mile to the main road and the long miles back to Dourados.

The old horse must have been five-hundred-years-old with terminal arthritis; he just wouldn't go faster than a snail going up a sandpaper hill. He'd take a step and then a little while later, another. But I usually had to remind him to take that second step. I finally gave him a kick with my heels, like you do with horses, and he actually took two-and a-half brisk steps before he decided that was enough of that. All day long we inched towards Dourados. Loide had made me a lunch of some barbequed beef and some hard bread which I ate throughout the day; my water bottle gave out long before mid afternoon. I'd whap the old horse and we'd quick-step two steps and then slow down to a speed which reminded me of old Dr Bill's unbelievably slow back-crawl.

We were still five miles out when the evening squadrons of parrots made their raucous announcement of impending pitch blackness. Just at dark the saddle slipped, and I fell onto the rocky road. It took me forever to put everything back on, and now the danged old horse was actually excited and acting frisky with all the saddle gear wrapped around his leg. Somehow we made it into Dourados about 9:30. I tied up old Stewball and brought some water out to him. The next day my balls were on fire; the second day they completely peeled for the first time, and then the skin dried and cracked and had to be very painfully peeled. Otherwise it got worse since as I moved, the now potato chip dry pieces of still attached skin would pull away from very tender spots; hundreds of very tender spots. The third and fourth day my testicles dried up, cracked and peeled... two or three times each day. Holy moly!

12 de Marco, 1968

Hi Love,

Ron Horton

Got a letter today, and also heard from Clara. I traded my bike for a horse and rode it 55 to 60 kilometers, about 35 miles. I have a 9 foot anaconda, who has bitten me three times. I had to buy bridles and all for the horse, but a man is loaning me a saddle. This same man has a short wave radio, and we can talk anytime you care......I've decided to enroll at Auburn whatever happens, even with the 75% certainty of being drafted....
Love,
Ron

22 de Marco, 1968

Hi,
Sorry I've been so bad about writing. I've been to Campo Grande and saw Janice off and am now back home. I received all the money, thanks. I think my weight's about the same; my hair is thinner. I'm hungry for biscuits, turnip greens, fried okra, cornbread, white-meat, and Southern fried chicken, big glass of iced tea, and that chocolate cake with sauce in the bottom.

You said you might be at Clara's when I get home. Is that Atlanta or New York? Thanks for the teaching forms. I might just teach if the war continues. Someone stole my briefcase, and the radio information; I guess it's useless. That's twice the guy isn't that cooperative also. I have three gardens: lettuce, cabbage, tomatoes, onions, broccoli, beets, radishes, cauliflower, eggplant, squash, corn, green beans, peas, celery, etc. It'll be producing in about a month. The horse is fine, and I'm learning to ride a little. Nothing else, so I'll close.

Love to all,
Ron

Seu Loide's cowboys had taught me to throw the bolas

Peace Corps Syndrome

to bring down cows and how to use the rawhide lariat I had watched one of the ranch hands make. The bolas had three stones, wrapped in rawhide on the end of six foot braids tied at the center. For the lariat, they'd take a just killed steer and cut a half-inch wide strip of its hide around the stomach and by rolling the steer back and forth they'd cut off enormously long strips. The Cavalheiro braided three of these strips, with all the hair and everything, and tied one end to a post in the ground. Then, he'd stretch the lariat he had just created as tightly as he could and throw a coil of old chain around the three braid strips, working the chain back and forth. The dagger and pistola in the sash around his waist, those classic Brazilian, wide topped, leather boots, and a big brimmed straw hat didn't slow him a bit as he pulled the chain tight along the stretched braid. He repeated this for several days, finally working it without soaking it twice a day. Soon the lariat was perfectly round, a beautiful affair, so stiff that when I said something about oiling it the Cavalheiro exploded, "Nunca, nunca, rapaz!" "It'll ruin it if you do. It has to stay stiff."

Now in the last few months of my two year Peace Corps stint I was staying with Vitor and Lydia and kept the old swayback either in the front yard or over at the Health Post's yard, tethered to graze. In the mornings, when I wasn't off with Vitor, I'd saddle the old horse whose mane was by now a bright red from the constantly blowing dust. I was so tall and lanky on the old swayback that my feet almost drug the ground. I had bought some cowboy boots and a bunch of tan Levis from another Peace Corps Volunteer just before he went back to the States.

The old horse and I would mope down to a soccer field a few blocks away on the edge of town, and I would practice throwing the lariat and the bolas. I had gotten a real wide double strip of rawhide that was a noise maker more than anything, but when I'd whack him just a little, the two stiff flaps would hit each other and crack like a whip. The horse would actually run a little this way as I flailed the lariat or the bolos around my head.

I preferred the bolos, all three of them between my fingers separating the two equal sized round rocks, bound in thick rawhide on double braids, and a third rock slightly larger and with a longer braid. Some threw the bolo holding the bigger stone in their hand while flinging the two smaller stones about six or seven feet away. Either way, once you started the stones moving a little above your head you had better have a perfect plan for releasing them, because if you didn't, you were going to get whacked. I mean you could get hurt, real quick and real bad.

Just in front of Vitor's house was a garage where he had his back up Kombi, complete with several engines in the process of being rebuilt by an alcoholic, but quite efficient mechanic. One day when my horse was tied up at a water trough in back of the garage the mechanic came out back to clean a sprayer that he had been using to paint the new back up Kombi, and being quite tight, he somehow missed the ground and instead sprayed the last of his blue paint on one side of my white horse. I jumped all over him, but the paint wasn't really all that thick, and I wound up laughing along with him. Big mistake!

The next week he was using green paint and thought it was just too bad that the horse's paint job was lopsided. When I rode my swaybacked, blue and green sided, white horse with the dust red mane and tail through town, legs almost dragging the ground, I must have made quite a picture, for gangs of kids would follow along for a block or two howling with laughter as I bounced along on my way to the bar or to the soccer field to practice being a cowboy. Little did I know that I was about to be a real rodeo cowboy.

Seu Lige (Say oh-Lee Gee) was a large landowner and another friend of some of my Brazilian pals, Victor Conde

Peace Corps Syndrome

and his family. Victor would drive us out on weekends to Seu Lige's ranch, about a three hour drive. Seu. Lige had a five room house, four with dirt floors, thousands of acres and thousands of Brahma cattle, pineapples in the back yard, and three or four Brazilian and Argentinean cowboys. One of the Argentinean cowboys used bolos in addition to the commonly used Brazilian leather lariats. The warmth and immediate acceptance by these people was like flood waters rushing over flat bottomland. Nothing was too pressing or important than to play or spend time doing <u>anything</u> <u>anyone</u> thought up. We would go out and let the ram, which had been a pet but had now grown huge, butt us or charge us. Juao would teach me to throw the bolas or the lariat. We'd shoot pistols. All the cowboys wore dirks or daggers, pistolas, and small silver embossed gourds with silver straws. They wore these gourds on their belts and used them to hold their hot tea or mate'. Mate' with at least three times the caffeine of espresso was brewed in each cowboy's gourd by pouring hot water over the mate' leaves. The brew was imbibed by sipping through a long silver straw with a fat bulbous teaspoon device on the end with dozens of small holes in it. The end with holes allowed the tea to be sucked into the straw while filtering out the leaves.

    Bottles of cognac or pinga were never far away, and at dusk little six-inch, homemade oil lamps made of tin with a finger grip and a cigarette sized wick coming out of a one inch tube, gave the only light. Just before dusk, thousands of parrots, three or four species in distinct flocks, flew just overhead creating a raucous sound equal to any heavy metal group's noise level. They flapped with short wings reminiscent of ducks. Then as darkness fell, with the jungle around us, the open fields allowed a zillion stars to appear, each brighter than our lamp, each square inch of the sky with more stars than I had ever seen in a North American sky, and they were all different from the stars I

Ron Horton

knew. No Orion's Belt, no Pleiades here. Then I saw the Southern Cross in the South American sky. It's like being on Mars or in a different galaxy when the stars are different. "Lions and tigers and bears. Oh My!"

One's first jungle sound assault, without lights, is unforgettable. There were screams, yelps, whistles, choruses, roars, moans, and buzzing, with most of those noises hitting you on the face, biting you on the butt, or crawling down your shirt.

There was a bunch of us that first night at Luige's; some of the guys slept on the porch, the women and kids got the house, and I slept in the corn crib on top of ten feet of unshucked corn. Only one problem as I tried to drop off to sleep, I could hear dozens of corn chewing critters munching away inches from my head. Sleep came hard that night; I sipped a little more cognac until I began to nod off and listened to the jungle sounds and looked up at the stars, so different, so much brighter, so many more.

I could have been on a planet only conceived in the mind of Edgar Rice Burroughs, with hundreds of his mythical, carnivorous, man chomping monsters, fighting and creating mayhem in the corn rat, chomping night. As the sun rose, I slowly came to life. Apparently, the mosquitoes, gnats, and other blood suckers had missed just enough of my life juices to allow me to crack open one eye lid through the cognac hang over. One sand papered eyeball peeped through the limbs of the corn crib to see thousands of scissor tailed fly-catchers descend into the one big tree in the middle of the yard, then seconds later all pop up again. Donna Loide came hip swaying across the yard, jet black hair shining, snow white teeth, nubile nipples perking through the thousand-time washed gossamer cotton, walked into the pineapple grove, squatted, and peed. For the first time in my life, I saw a woman urinate. Shazam! For a 23 year old, this was exciting stuff.

She was an uncompromising flirt to me, and this was not

Peace Corps Syndrome

good as Seu Lige had just liberated Donna Loide from her first husband, and threats and raids and guns had been used in several exchanges. Seu Lige had nubs for most of his fingers, he had the type of jungle rot we call leprosy, but it was in remission then.

There was a bad dry season that year, and before I met Seu Lige, Vitor had told me about him and about all the cattle he was loosing. After I got to know Lige and visited his place several times, riding to my hearts content on the horse of my choice, I began to notice an unusual feature of his giant ranch. Every hundred yards or so there'd be a clump of trees amid the beginnings of the Pantanal, a lowland savannah with natural ponds spotted across the land, like mosquito bites on my arms. These water holes had dried up, but walking down into one I could see that just inches down there was damp mud. My god I thought, all he's got to do is dig a couple of these out and he'd have water. Lige lost a lot of cows that year.

27 de Janeiro, 1968
Hi,
I've been bird trapping lately, caught one that is worth 50-150 mil (10-30 days pay for me). It all depends if he turns out to be a good singer; you use them to call and catch others. Hope the flu has run its course, and you are back on the golf course. Let's see, went to Dourados' 1st Beer Festival, where my sunglasses and beer mug were stolen and almost the Jeep. I went outside to get some air, saw a guy giving the Jeep the once over, and when he got inside it, I grabbed him by the back of the neck and threw him on the pavement and called the police, who came about 5 minutes later, all the time with me holding him.... I'm going to see if I can terminate early to get into Auburn in Sept., if not I'll extend two to three months so I can enter without having to worry about the draft.
Much love. See you soon,

Ron Horton

Ron

Vitor got real excided about catching these solid black, singing birds called Bicudos, each worth about a months wages i.e. 200,000 cruzeiros. Soon, he and I were out in the (varjao) brushy country with his mist net, so transparent that birds fly right into it. Vitor had borrowed a friend's male Bicudo in his beautiful hand made bird cage with three smaller capture cages on the sides. The male Bicudos were very territorial and sang such beautiful songs that Brazilians had made entire LP albums of their music. Vitor said the music was so complex that nothing was repeated in the entire album. We set the cages out beside some 12 feet high brush and went off to set the mist net. Soon the caged Bicudo was singing his little ass off and like magic a wild bird showed up almost immediately. The three smaller, capture cages opened on the top and side with little spring loaded devices that closed the little six-inch by four-inch doors made of ¼-inch wood, with wire between. The theory was that the wild bird would try to get to the caged bird and hop into the traps. Of course, the wild bird hopped on every inch of the cages, except the trip set on the floor of the capture cage. After we went back to the mist net we had to spend a good half hour releasing dozens of small birds, most of which I had never seen, but no Bicudos. Vitor was greatly disappointed.

I came back with him one day and stopped off at Seu Loide's while he went on to Maracaju, giving me about two hours to try to trap the Bicudo. I had brought along the same caged bird set up we had used before and quickly set it up across the creek from the rice fields. I was grinning so horrendously from ear to ear when Vitor returned and slowed to ford the 25-foot wide creek that he knew that I had been successful.

At the time I was staying in Dourados with Seu Liege at his new townhouse, and I set my new Bicudo in the back

Peace Corps Syndrome

where I had a cot on the patio. After a couple of days getting accustomed to his surroundings, the big beaked bird began to sing this beautiful song; I had grown up around a Canary and loved to hear a songbird. The next day when I came home Liege sadly told me the bird had escaped. I really think he let it go on purpose.

Macumba

Macumba is Brazil's equivalent of voodoo, oddly, a subject I had written a research paper on in 1966 before entering Peace Corps. However, when I first became acquainted with Macumba, I didn't realize that it was voodoo. Halfway through Peace Corps training the teachers and older PCV'S threw us a Brazilian party full of samba music, black beans and rice, and pinga or cachacha, the 100% corn liquor and national drink of Brazil. I ate my first mandioca, the poisonous root that is de-toxified by boiling and then fried and is the most delicious bread like substance on earth. After a slick desert called flan, a black American ex-PCV in white pants and a blousy white shirt announced that he was going to perform a Macumba ceremony. I wish I had realized at the time that the guy was actually doing a voodoo ceremony with some statues of saints, Mary, some Indians and a bunch of candles. He smoked a cigar and drank some booze, and I didn't think much about it until one day a year-and-a-half later when I realized that all my Brazilian friends were involved in Macumba and actively going to the voodoo churches.

Seu Lige first told me his story out at his ranch. I knew a little about it from Vitor, how Lige had stolen this beauty from a real poor subsistence farmer and that death threats had ensued from the jilted lover. Sumi was a beauty by frontier standards that included dozens of infected insect bite scars on her legs, but still a saucy, sweet woman who flirted outrageously with me. As mentioned before, most of Lige's finger tips were gone due to his leprosy which was in remission. The Peace Corps doctor, Bill _____, had given me the okay when Lige and Sumi invited me to live with them in their new big house in town.

It was on one of our week-end jaunts out to the ranch that a young friend of Vitors from Sao Paulo came by bus in response to an appeal by Lige. That this 25-year-old guy could be a famous Macumba priest was the furthest thing from my mind as I walked along with the group, listening to them talking until I heard enough to figure out that something was going on, and I began my usual string of questions. Just then the young priest, Roberto, walked straight over to where the road came into the yard proper. He looked around and spotting an old shovel, walked back to the packed dirt, dug down about a foot and discovered a black chicken feather wrapped in plastic, an apparent voodoo curse. "Bad Macumba," he expounded, holding it toward Lige. "Someone has put a black curse on you".

Lige was taking an unbelievable number of injections daily for god knows what besides the leprosy. Brazilians on the frontier refused to take pills or capsules; one of the missionaries took so many injections for everything that he had reactions constantly. So Roberto removed the curse on Lige by destroying the black feather and doing a little ceremony. I totally dismissed all this as hogwash until three days later, back at Lydia's house, when Roberto had a talk with Lydia's cousin who had just arrived from Rio. Her cousin had been having a lot of inexplicable medical problems and was desperate because of his failing health. Within minutes of his arrival, Roberto named a woman's name that only the cousin knew, a woman he had gotten pregnant and abandoned. Everybody was flabbergasted by Roberto miraculously coming up with the girl's name. He did a ceremony to do away with the black Macumba curse and the cousin got better from that moment on.

Peace Corps Syndrome

It was at about this time that I went to my first real voodoo church; Lydia, Vitor, Pule, Roberto and I walked up to the board and bat, wooden house only two blocks from Vitor's. As we entered, seven or eight women in big flowing skirts and loose white blouses, scarves around their heads, waited while we took our shoes off at the back and then one by one we were cleansed. Thank god, I didn't have to go first. Lydia was led a few feet toward the front while another small group poured something on the floor into a circle with a star in the middle and lit what was obviously gunpowder. The other group of women now began to dance around Lydia and chant while they moved their fingers all around her body, inches away, in a constant swaying movement occasionally throwing their fingers to the ceiling as if expelling any evil spirits from her body. They spent three or four minutes on each one of us before they let us sit down. When my time came I could feel their 50 fingers like a tingle or the goose bumps though they never touched me. Then one of the women began chanting to a table filled with dozens of statues and candles. There were several such tables of Catholic and Indian statues. We had arrived just before the evening service.

Suddenly a very black man walked out into the room and began smoking an enormous cigar, walking around and gesturing to some of the statues. He picked up a new bottle of cachacha and began to chug-a-lug while puffing like "the little engine that could" on the cigar. He did this for quite a while until he started wailing and reeling, going into his Macumba trance. He got so snockered that he was rolling on the floor. Lydia had told me before that they believed that no one had gotten to heaven yet, except the two or three taken directly there in the Bible, that all others were in transit and couldn't get there until they helped many of us back on earth, i.e. helping do good Macumba. The priests in their trances could interact with different spirits to help figure out bad Macumba spells or help in other ways. Some priests had favorite spirits they could easily contact, but sometimes new spirits would jump in to visit and help, or not. The priest went into a squatting, slow kicking dance with almost bloated fish-like eyes in his trance, so glazed was he. The priestess had to follow him around as he rolled on the floor to pick up all the messages for the different requests from the congregation that night.

PROSTITUTES

Prostitutes in Brazil were as numerous as grains of sand on a beach. By Brazilian moral standards, men married around the age of thirty-five to an eighteen to twenty-year-old virgin. If the bride was not a virgin, well out she went. One of our Peace Corps language teachers, a Brazilian, told us wild stories about all the anally promiscuous girls from Rio, who were most chic, having years of anal sex until they married, whereupon they were still vaginal virgins, but back to Brazilian morals. In Dourados, a town of 10,000 people, electricity, running water, streets about to be paved, there were eight to ten blocks of wall to wall "zona" houses, and several out on the edge of the jungle, where you could see the mayor, all the doctors, and almost every guy from town, parked in front of double, triple wide open doors. There were painted women, with samba music on a record player, festoons of party lights, and four or five women sitting around on a sofa. A guy could go window shopping and select from literally hundreds of women. Brazilians are a Portuguese, Indian, African mix resulting in every variation of color: black, brown, cream or earthy. Some were obviously very young Indian girls.

I made about $35 to $45 American a month, or 150,000 to 200,000 Brazilian dollars or cruzerios. The average pay for a Brazilian was about $600 a year. That comes to about 5000 Brazilian dollars or $1.50 American a day. You could

Peace Corps Syndrome

get a prostitute for 5000 cruzeinos...expensive cigarettes cost 2000 cruzeinos a pack. So, you could window shop and have sex with your selection of the evening for the equivalent of two and a half packs of cigarettes.

Part of my job in Dourados as a medical lab tech was to see that the working girls had their government health cards up to date. Prostitution was legal, but required a health card, and we checked for syphilis and gonorrhea at the Health Post. AIDS was, of course, unknown at the time.

One horny afternoon, soon after a payday actually arrived, at a new house in the zona, I found Sarah, 24, blondish and pretty, and she spoke fairly good English! We had sex three or four times over several months and talked. She had been raised by American missionaries. Virtually every family I knew in Brazil had a young girl or two, passed on to foster homes to rear as servants, literally so they wouldn't starve to death. Life is hard on the Mato Grossan Frontier. Many such girls were regularly molested when they got to the age where they would be dating or wanting to date. In a couple of families I knew, this peaking pubescence seemed to spark into the girl becoming sexually active, and once the wife of the house knew, immediately, the girl was out the door. The girl could then either get married, if she was lucky, or be forced into prostitution. There were few jobs for young girls with no skills. I'm sure many eventually met husbands as customers in the brothels. Sarah had a boy-friend she told me about, and they had plans they apparently had made.

Hell, I was a young man, hormones raging, living around a gorgeous thirty-five-year old Peace Corps nurse, and constantly horny. I couldn't afford to visit more than once or twice each 60 day period. Good customers would come, sit with and buy the girls two or three drinks, and then go out back. None of the rooms had ceilings. They were big open buildings with six to nine foot rooms consisting of walls and a curtain...some without doors.

You could hear lots of other sounds. Being a 23-year-old string bean, cheapskate customer, the women would make quick money with me.

One hilarious adventure occurred just as our Peace Corps group arrived in Rio. In those innocent days of the late 1960's, we parted hard and bed hopped with all the gusto of Bacchus reincarnated as a Shriner. We were a tight-knit group, some of the best camaraderie of my life. Four or five of us guys were aware that our youngest male, Dan_____ was still a virgin, and Rio's clubs were stocked with thousands of the most gorgeous, voluptuous, young, legal prostitutes in the world. Every complexion, every shade God ever made, and this in the pre HIV age of innocence. So four of us checked out Dan as he dressed to go out as a boy and return as a man. Actually, we missed the real drama. At about 1:30 in the morning an extremely distraught young man walked into our room where we were drinking.

Dan had gone out by himself to the clubs and window shopped among the elite beauties of the world, most with waist length hair...pleasure toys from paradise. Dan had chosen the most ravishing one of all, he told us, and had brought her back to his room to consummate the deal. It seems they had made-out a bit in the club and then in his room, then with the lights off, Dan and the beauty undressed, and Dan made ready to become a man with a man.

The beautiful lady he had selected was a male, one of Rio's famous transvestites. Rio has thousands of idle, rich transvestites who have outrageous full dress ball in the National Theatre. I really don't think it's humanly possible to describe the expression on Dan's face or the tone in his voice as he described the experience. I later heard he had saved face and lost his virginity with the daughter of the governor of the state of Amazonia.

Peace Corps Syndrome

ADVENTURES WITH BRAZIL'S ELI WHITNEY

Antonio Barreto was the John Deere, Cyrus McCormick and Eli Whitney of Brazil all rolled into one when I met him in 1968 at a rodeo in Maracaju, Mato Grosso. Maracaju was at the end of Vitor's local bus line which he made from Dourados each day in his VW bus called a Kombi. Vitor and Lydia had arrived in Dourados from the much older and heavily populated state of Sao Paulo and the little city of Avare.

Antonio had developed the very first brush hog or giant lawn mower for ranchers in the country after he had traveled to the USA and toured several old agricultural museums. One odd thing about a third world country like Brazil was that you just didn't see any old vehicles sitting around. They were just too valuable and irreplaceable like they are now in Cuba. They always seemed to be able to fix them up and drive them somehow. Anyhow, Antonio had developed a fantastic machine made from old differentials or rear ends out of old cars that he could scrounge up. Almost immediately he had to start making his own differentials. He had replaced the car wheels with giant, six-foot metal, rolled edge jobs with six-inch teeth for traction, put a four-foot solid arm on the sawed-off drive shaft with two three-foot swing blades off the solid one, put a hitch up front, and he had the baddest-ass brush hog that you could pull with everything from oxen to tractors. It would cut everything up to about four inches in diameter, a perfect machine to maintain pasture, a great way not to have to burn the fields every year.

Antonio was in his 40's, and I was 24; both of us full of brass, beans and bull or however you want to say that we both had an unusual zeal that resulted in the two of us having marvelous adventures from the moment we met. Antonio had brought a big truck full of his machines to

Maracaju for the week long event from about a thousand miles away. He was demonstrating his devices at several ranches each day and selling them like hotcakes. He soon had Vitor really interested in thinking about selling them for a living.

Vitor and Antonio had been raised together back in Avare, and while Vitor and I waited the two-and-a-half hours before the bus route back to Dourados pulled us away, the three of us eased over to the arena to watch part of the week long cowboy shindig. We passed some of the most unusual cattle I had ever seen, some massively thick bulls with legs so short you could reach down and scratch their backs, other pens had Santa Gertrudis and Charolais, which some like my friend Al were using to cross with the native Brahma cattle.

The rodeo cowboys were a pretty raw looking bunch of bronco riding, cachaxa drinking, roustabouts. We watched as they unloaded the wild broncos they would later try to ride or rope as we sat at a group of little tables set under some welcoming giant figueira trees. The bleachers were on the other side of the arena as were the gates for releasing the wild horses and their riders. It was a regular, ride the wild horse event open to any and all riders. Vitor still had a good while before we had to take the Kombi back home. As the rodeo announcer on a small amplifier awarded the prizes for breaking horses, he started talking about a "Brahma Beast from Hell" that had never been ridden throughout dozens of rodeos back in the heavily populated states that included the mega-cities of Sao Paulo and Rio, and most of the south of the country. It was the size of a good horse, a Brahma with an enormous hump and those ears as big as an elephants, but not a bull and no mean looking horns. The announcer went on and on as we drank beer under the figueira trees daring anyone to dare to ride the beast. Then he got my attention when he said there was a quarter of a million Brazilian dollar prize ($50 US), but a full months pay to me and most of the folks in the stands. Antonio kept looking over at me and grinning with a little teasing laugh whenever the guy talked about the "can't be ridden beast."

   Finally I walked around the entire arena to the pen to take a good look at the creature which didn't look too lethal. So I walked back to the announcer's stand and asked the head of the rodeo if I could take a shot at riding the Brahma. I should have skee-dattled when that "Aha, another idiot to be trampled to dust in the Roman Circus" grin enveloped his blushing, exuberant countenance and ran over his increasingly red cheeks. He walked over to the loading chute gesturing and hollering to the hands to bring the wild beast hither before walking back up to the steps to the announcer's platform. Then he got back on the loudspeaker to get the crowds' attention as two cowboys on horses and five or six other hands opened and closed a gate, and I found myself climbing the eight-foot tall, wooden slat fence as the rodeo hands were cinching the Brahma's head in tight. Others were passing a cinch around the beast's belly.

   I had never seen a cinch and suddenly found myself with both hands (no single handed rules here) between two leather straps, one with sheepskin on it. I sat there only a very few seconds before the rodeo boss looked straight into my eyes. I gave him a nod and the gate flew open and the critter started showing why it had never been ridden. It jumped 15-feet straight up and spun 20 or 30 times so fast that I went flying, and I mean really flying, and whammed down on what was, thank god, fairly soft, horse churned-up ground. I was hurt too. The cinch had been so tight that the centrifugal force had almost pulled the meat off my fingers; it felt so bad. Antonio and Vitor were roaring as I walked back over across the rodeo floor.

   I got several good slaps on the back and another big lukewarm beer. Another hour went by and as the afternoon wore on and no one else had tried to ride the Brahma, Antonio began to talk about his wild, earlier days when he had actually ridden some in rodeos, "Ronaldo, olhe aqui rapaz" "You would have stayed on if you had locked your elbows into your hip bones and kept them there". What the hell, 24-years-old and full of mainly vinegar, I walked back over to the rodeo boss and asked if I could try again. "Certo" he replied.

This time as they brought the Brahma back into the loading chute I had a couple of mechanic's rags to go over the pair of gloves I had used on the first attempt. The rodeo hands tightened the cinch unbelievably tighter this time than last; once again the head honcho waited till I had stopped moving and looked at him. This time when I nodded I guess I was a little more prepared because as the Brahma began his high altitude assault on gravity, I actually stayed on. We sailed and soared and spun this way, with forelegs skimming the ground every ten to twenty feet; then the crazed creature from hell sailed completely backwards with me on top seemingly immune to the laws of gravity until we came down real hard from what seemed like a good ten-feet up in the air. My right leg was trapped under the horse sized Brahma, my hands were being torn off by the cinch which was tightened in a great burst of searing pain as the hell-beast thrashed with all its legs and weight, but my hands would not come out of the cinch. With my leg under it, I pulled with all my strength to free my hands, but neither one of us could do anything but thrash on the ground. The rodeo hands finally got to me. I was in such pain that I was screaming in English, **"My hands, my hands!"**

Two guys grabbed the Brahma's head…others pulled me off as somebody finally got the cinch loosened. It appeared to all that I had wrestled the beast to the ground and held it there. **I was a rodeo hero!!** *(40 years later, I have serious problems of all sorts with my fingers and*

Peace Corps Syndrome

hands somewhat attributable to just how badly hurt I was by that cinch tightening on my hands).

They had a big ceremony at the grandstand, the rodeo boss on the microphone obviously really pissed that he had to give me the money. He started rattling on just before he turned on the mike that I was an American ringer who had won some money two years before, but I just looked at him with my famous shit-eating grin. So he had no choice but to give me the money, a humongous stack of bills, since the largest denomination then was a 5000 cruzeiro note and most notes were singles. I had won a quarter of a million! He handed me the cash after going on for several minutes about what a big deal it was, to have ridden the Brahma. Later when I actually counted the money, I found he had stiffed me thirty-five thousand Brazilian dollars. . .

15 de Junho, 1968
Hi Family,

I'm about 90 km. from Dourados in Maracatu at a county fair. I'm helping Victor sell mowers to ranchers and he has made about $3000 this week. I've met the owner of the factory that makes the machine and after a week, he offered me my choice of any state in the Amazon region. It would do for $500-$2000/month, and as you know by now, is a lot of money here in Brazil.

I'm a hero? these days. I rode a Brahma (never broken) in the Rodeo they have here, fell off, rode again and stayed on even when he fell (on top of me). I'm o.k. except for my hands; they're like raw meat as they were trapped under the cinch when I fell. I won 200 cruzeiros (as much as I earn in a month) and had a chance at 500 or more, but I don't think I can ride this afternoon. We'll see. My wrist is sprained or chipped. Everything else is fine. Peace Corps and I are at each other's throats. The kid head of the state

got sassy (in letter) and I told him how and what to do with his office and various body parts. Only 1 1/2- 2 months. Love to all. See you soon.
over.....
Please excuse the dirt, but I've been traveling. Am doing many things, enjoying myself most of the time. Really missing home. Picking up as many animal skins as I can. Ocelot, Jaguar, Anaconda, Boa Constrictor, Anteater. I'll be home in less than two months.

Helped a guy make about $4000 last week, and I've been offered a position doing the same work, exhibiting giant lawn mowers (Bushmasters) that sell for 3 million cruzeiros, and of which I earn 30 %. We've sold about 20 (Only awaiting shipments to close deals now). I might have to look into this.

If you're rich at the moment and won't need your loot for about two months, let me know, I'd like to bring many things back (presents), but also to sell such as leather and animal skins. If I can find and buy, I could make several thousand dollars with just a little cash. I'll be getting about 2-3 hundred here in one month, and the rest 4-5 hundred when I get to New York. Ask Ann if she'd like a jaguar or ocelot coat or rug etc.
Love, Ron

My adventures with Antonio got a lot better from that moment on. The day after the rodeo we delivered a couple of brush hogs to big fazendas. While we were there unloading, Antonio began asking about special places to see and that's how we heard about the giant sinkholes and the caves. The next day found us fifty miles further out in the wild on the 40 degree talus slope of a very unusual sinkhole. We parked his 2 ½ ton Ford flatbed at the end of a trail (we had gotten very specific directions) and walked

Peace Corps Syndrome

down a steep slope for quite a ways before the steepest incline began, and there were several hundred yards of it. We would walk and slide at little diagonals, grabbing limbs of the little trees that grew at wild angles since most were losing the fight with gravity.

About 75 feet from the bottom I saw the most unusual geographic formation of my life, and I've seen quite a few. There in the bottom were two crystal clear bottomless pools, each 35-45 feet across and separated by a single rock shelf directly across but still two feet under the clear as air water. You could see forever straight down, with the midday tropical sun spotlighting all the way down to China, and you could see past that into further depths. Then we saw the critters... giant blue crabs almost identical to the big ones on the Gulf Coast, only larger. I saw several of what appeared to be snakes, but I recognized them as legless sirens, or amphiumas, types of amphibians I had just studied in biology the year before.

Lots of little minnows skittered around everywhere as Antonio and I stripped and eased into the water to cool off and explore. Where we entered was the only place in the big oblong bottom where one could easily crawl in or out without climbing up some loose rocks that sloped almost straight down the last hundred yards to the rim of the pool. It was real eerie, immediately, just like when I jumped over the side of a 50 foot sloop a hundred miles off Mobile, Alabama, becalmed in what the charts showed to be 5000 feet of water just past the continental shelf.

Antonio and I made it to the middle and sat on the bench for a few minutes. The blue crabs were everywhere where the water was a few feet deep, and there were six to eight on the shelf. The snake like sirens swam away from me as I swam on to the far side. I saw no large fish or obvious food for the big crabs. There were by now, however, gathering swarms of little guppy sized fish around me. When I reached the far bank and stopped, standing on a ledge looking behind me into the crystal clear abyss that was mesmerizing and increasingly unsettling, I felt something nibbling on my fingers. When I pulled my left hand out of the water there were two to four fish on each finger, bizarrely attached to my cuticles, apparently so hungry they were T-bone steak material. I had to shake them off. Just then Antonio joined me, a strange look on his face. I put my hands back under water, and just as he settled in on arrival, I pulled both hands from the water and there were 15 to 20 small fish attached to each hand.

Without a sound Antonio and I quietly scratched and crawled up the loose talus in front of us, not an easy thing. The feeling that some creature or creatures were below was so overwhelming that I wouldn't have re-entered the water for all the money in the world. The study of herpetology was so young in Mato Grosso that the books I had didn't list any sirens or salamanders. Now after years of working with endangered species with the U.S. Fish and Wildlife, I realize that those creatures could have been unique, unreported new species or sub-species. Shazam!!

The second sinkhole was several hours away and was called the Burracao, or giant hole. Word was that no one had ever gone down into the crater-like jungle scene. Antonio had "haruumphed" back at the fazenda when the local rancher had told us this, so I wasn't surprised when we stopped on the way out of town and Antonio bought 200 meters of 3/4 inch rope…a bit over 600 feet.

We secured the rope to a little sloping bench just at the edge of Edgar Rice Burrough's imagination. The sinkhole was about a half mile across and enormously deep, the sides straight down forever into the tops of giant tropical mahoganies and figueiros (fig trees) that were dwarfed down below perhaps by what was the most lush and greenest jungle I have seen. Sheer rock was evident all around the sides of the Burracao. When we first walked up and began to work tying the rope, we saw and heard two pair of macaws down on the forest canopy, a good 500 feet down. They had started flying around the rim of the hole and were fussing, a beautiful red-blue-yellow pair and a blue and yellow pair.

While we worked, I had noticed the birds every few minutes on the far side and a little higher up. I couldn't see them during half their big circular flight as they were under the cliff-edge we were standing on as we threw the rope over. Long time going down! Just as we got a little gear together and were commenting that it looked like the rope hadn't quite reached the bottom, the two pair of macaws burst out of the trees at the cliff edge only ten or twelve feet away, flying straight at us and screaming like banshees from hell. They flew only three or four feet over our heads twice and then went off into the greenness. They were obviously nesting down in the bottom where it appeared no terrestrial footed or hoofed animal could ever go except by falling in the seemingly inaccessible sinkhole.

We inched down the rope, me first, using rocks and a little jungle along the way to kind of walk our way down with our gloved hands on the rough rope. It really felt like deepest Africa, but this was on the Brazilian frontier where no one besides the indigenous Indian tribes had entered and explored until the late 1950's, and this was 1968. The ropes gave out about 15 feet above the boulder strewn bottom of the phenomenally huge, green, cone shaped hole. There was a semblance of a small game trail for a few yards but it trickled off into a bamboo grove, the common variety about four to six inches across, with horribly sharp thorns on three sides of each 12 to14-inch section of the 40 foot tall groves. The thorns were only ¾ to one-inch long thorns but 2½-inches across at the base…obscenely shaped nightmares of nature, short but with the capability to stop an elephant… or any damn thing.

Most of the floor was the dense, verdant green of jungle giants, some with enormously wide root spreads at the bottom like giant inverted flying buttresses of Notre Dame Cathedral, only upside down, the trees held upright in the nutrient weak shallow soil. Here all the nutrients were stored in the tree and not in the soil like in the temperate USA. We saw no sign of big animals, no tracks, nests or spoor. There was no chance of spotting the macaw's nests because the foliage was so unbelievably dense. No sign of man anywhere and the local legend was that no one had ever gone to the bottom before. Perhaps we were the first humans to tread there.

The next morning we went to several spots where no human had certainly ever walked or been. We drove to Fiolandia, with two stores and a bar-restaurant-pensao, and got a room for the night and ordered carne assada (meat roasted) on spits and continually served while one cut off only the fire cooked outside, then the waiters would put the spit back over the hot coals for another five minutes or so. Meals were long drawn out celebrations of leisurely conversation and lukewarm beers. After about two of the almost quart sized beers, Antonio offered me a job selling bush hogs. He guaranteed me $500 US minimum a month; I later saw Vitor make three times that in two days. Antonio said that he would provide a truck and offered me the giant island at the mouth of the Amazon, Marahao, as part of my territory. His offer got my interest. Particularly, months later in the state of Sao Paulo when I saw his foundry that he had built from scratch, a 50 foot tall smelter and foundry, a building wing with ten to twelve metal lathes machining the gears he had made from scrap metal and some iron ore and limestone. Other buildings manufactured the wheels and put the differentials together.

Our limestone sinkhole adventures were not over by a long shot. There was yet a third mysterious place to go explore, a large underground lake with an enormous open canopy ten times bigger than the Hollywood Bowl. So,

Peace Corps Syndrome

after the great times with the blue crabs and sirens, we found ourselves walking down a long slope reminiscent of the last descent into the unknown. Way down at the bottom we could see the beginning of the lake just at the edge of full sunlight. The water was so clear, however, that we found ourselves knee deep in cool water before we realized it, backing out and looking in the receding blackness of a large lake that disappeared into god knows what. We tossed several rocks way back before starting back up; there didn't seem to be any adventure here until we walked back up to where the cave went down to the left. As we got over toward this descending slope, crunching sounds bought our attention to the ground. "Meus deus" spouted Antonio. I picked up a handful of the material, and it was nothing but little-bitty bat skulls and bones. You couldn't see any signs of guano, so we quickly realized that it had been a long time since they had lived here; then we saw why. The entire large sloping cave had filled up all voids from both directions. From the ceiling, 2 ½ to 3 foot long, finger sized stalactites dripped every 6 to 8 inches and hung down to within inches of billions of the wee bat bones several feet deep.

Looking down to where the sloping cave disappeared a hundred feet or more, I could see what might be a way around the lake, so I decided to go down. I slid off, kicking the stalactites out of the way as I went, breaking hundreds of them as dozens of little bat bones got into my socks and everywhere up and down my pants and shirt. Down and down I went to the bottom where I soon found out the trip was a waste of time for further caving. I thought it would be an easy task going back up, but I immediately found out the bat bones were too loose to allow traction. I tried and tried, finally pumping my legs to exhaustion and starting to get concerned. Finally, I stood up as straight as I could and by pressing my back against the razor sharp stalactite stubs I could move my legs uphill a foot at a time. Then I'd have to push up with my by now bleeding back. It was a long and strange trip up the football field length slope, wallowing in three feet of long dead creatures who had left their bones for me to swim in.

Antonio didn't start laughing until I was all the way back up. I was so filthy and sore that the lake below called me back down for a swim and to cool off. Just as I got out of the water and Antonio was 20 feet up the slope, I threw one long last rock, missing the domed top where the last reflected light barely showed the ceiling. Just as I turned to climb out, the rock hit and its splash reflected just enough light for me to see a far back wall. We obviously didn't have good sense as Antonio and I turned and swam across the lake into a midnight void from where you could look down through the crystal clear water and see rocks on the bottom, 30 or 40 feet below and about a hundred feet from the shore.

Then the water got pitch black! I'll never forget that moment when we slowly dogpaddled up to what turned out to be a ledge. Turning and looking back into the light of the domed entrance wasn't so bad, but looking down was. Neither of us wanted to wake up the giant beast lurking just under our feet. We hung on to the ledge briefly before turning and quietly easing our way around the side to the shore. Another long sigh of relief.

It was now only a few weeks until I left Brazil, so I let my new friend kidnap and take me 1500 miles back east to his home town of Avare, Sao Paulo. There I saw the first TV sets I'd seen in two years. Antonio had a beautiful young wife and a young child; his wife watched Brazilian soaps that had a lot of bedroom scenes as I remember.

Antonio's factory was impressive with buildings which housed banks of lathes, a rolling mill and a foundry. The finished product had five-foot-tall, metal wheels with spokes, a truck differential which drove the cutting blades,

Peace Corps Syndrome

all covered by a thick metal cage. He had been so successful that two other good sized factories had stolen his idea and were in full production.

We loaded eight bush hogs on the big flatbed truck and headed back to Dourados to deliver them to Vitor, who by now was in the process of selling his bus line, so lucrative was the future in selling the bush hogs. All the roads were dirt and real rough; a lot of washboard road we called it, so regular were the ruts...a beautiful word in Portuguese, trepidacao. When Antonio got tired and had me drive, I shifted through the gears and got up to about 25 mph, breaking for the deeper holes. He kept trying to get me to go faster until finally he reached over with his silver toed boot and mashed my foot all the way down to the floor and kept it there. "Vai encima!!" Which means, get on top of it!

Soon I had the truck skimming at 60 mph over a road so rough that we were literally airborne most of the time. The two-and-a-half ton truck was loaded with eight of those big old machines on the back, their long front tongues sticking 12 to 15 feet up above the truck bed; we were flying along. We'd hit a particularly big one I just couldn't miss every so often, and the truck would fly 20 to 30 feet before one or two of our 10 wheels would alight to kiss the inch-deep red dust as we tore across Brazil leaving a cloud behind that spread as fast as a nuclear explosion's burst. So many thousands of times since then since I never saw him again, I have heard him say, "Vai encima rapaz, vai encima!"

I lost one of my life's best friends and true entrepreneurial colleagues when the draft board got on my tail almost immediately after this period. Antonio had offered me $500 US a month, plus commission, which could have been $5000 to $10,000 per month. I have never had the opportunity to make that kind of money since that time. I would have been traveling around the mouth of the Amazon. Just as I was leaving the country, Vitor told me

Ron Horton

Ford Motor had gone in with Antonio to make differentials for the soon to be opened truck factory only a few miles away from Avare.

Rob the Troubadour

Rob always reminded me of one of the Kingston Trio. His upper arms were proportionally a little too short for him to be a model for a Greek statue so that short sleeve shirts hung down onto his forearms. He wasn't what I'd call handsome, but maybe good looking to a girl due to his good natured grin, a great personality and guitar ability. At 5' 9" or so, I never saw him take an interest in the ladies until the long legged, gorgeous Doctora Roberta, a psychiatrist from Rio, came along.

In the mid 1960's, folk singing was a major past time at any gathering, so during our Peace Corps training having three guitar players in our group wasn't out of the ordinary. Rob played a mean guitar, and his voice didn't hurt too bad, so when he'd start getting out his beautiful old Martin I'd start ambling over. Rob had a great sense of humor and

Peace Corps Syndrome

an ability to get me and other saps to sing along. He was a naturally sweet guy as were almost all of my Peace Corps pals. During Peace Corps training we were supposed to all go together to the Amazon Basin, but as I have mentioned before, I was kidnapped and sent down to the Paraguayan border, and didn't expect to see him again for a long time. However, we corresponded and planned a jungle cruise in 1967 for our gang at our mid-service, two week vacation on the Amazon River up around Manaus. Peace Corps screwed up, as usual, when it came to paying us on time or at all, so I wasn't able to meet Rob, Dan and the gals, because I didn't have enough money except to go visit Dr. Bill in Campo Grande for a few days. The others had an enormously good time on their Amazon cruise, and I was quite peeved for a while, until Peace Corps tried to atone for their negligence in leaving dozens of us without money for over three months (twice), and flew the lot of us to Rio for Carnival in 1968.

We all stayed at the Hotel Florida and hung out together, and being on Rio per diem, we could afford to spend two or three dollars American on a meal. This meant we could afford to hit all the top restaurants, so almost every evening we'd go out to eat and then come back to the hotel before taking the wild bus rides or cabs to downtown. There were dozens of revelers drinking and doing the Samba and dancing, the guys using boxes of wooden matches to shake for rhythm. One fellow bus partier had one of those strange drum like devices, so common during Carnival, with some kind of push and pull handle inside that made sounds like banshees.

The fantastically wide, hand-laid tile sidewalks with sweeping swirls of white and grey lead the poorer folk to walk downtown or toward the beaches where hundreds of favela (slum) folk were lighting candles at Macumba shrines or pushing three-feet-long, two-foot-high boats made of paper and filled with lighted candles into the surf.

Ron Horton

Once off the bus we had to walk about five blocks to the bleachers for the Samba School shows. Each Samba School consisted of 5,000 to 12,000 of Rio's slum dwellers dressed in fantastic costumes of feathers or rhinestones, or just about nothing. These folks would spend most of their year's salaries on their outfits for Carnival. Making the costumes and floats would consume most of their nights at their neighborhood, barn like, Samba School headquarters. Their very essence and social lives were meshed in their year's creation of new songs, dances, and themes for their three or four hours of glory as they marched through the main boulevard of Rio de Janerio

One night as we walked down from the viewing stands in downtown Rio, after watching several Samba Schools go by in festoons of color with lots of skin and body parts bouncing and weird instruments honking, Natalie Wood and a small entourage crossed in front of us going in the opposite direction. She and Robert Wagner had just divorced, so I guess she was cruising. She was gone before I could go, "Gollee!" like Gomer Pyle.

In the early afternoons, when we crawled out of our alcoholic daze, Rob and I, usually with Charles or Dan, maybe Helen and Glenda would wind up at some sidewalk café for a little lunch. Rob always seemed to pull his guitar out of thin air, and off we'd go across the coastal front highway to the beaches. Rio's beaches during Carnival are a Bacchanalian orgy of the celebration of being alive, all inhibitions out the door…there were couples making out everywhere. But Carnival was soon over, and we all went back to our sites for the agonizingly slow second year of service.

I didn't write any of my friends up north in the Amazon that last year, but arriving in Rio for the third time almost a year later was as exciting as the first two times, and I immediately bumped into my old Milwaukee trained Amazon bunch of revelers. I was freaking out so much about the draft that I proposed to Glenda within an hour of seeing her again, "Marry me to keep me from the nightmare of Viet Nam," I implored, but she and Helen both turned me down, but they still liked me enough to sleep with me several times in the next few days. Peace Corps nookie in the sixties was innocent, carefree and somehow sweeter than those sexually wild days of the 1970's.

I was soon hanging out with Dan, Rob, Nora and Chris to the point where we actually considered traveling back to the States together by way of Machu Pichu via Montivideo and Buenos Aires. That was actually our second idea. Nora had come up with the idea of sailing back. This would have been right in the middle of the hurricane season, Dohhh!! That idea got as far as going out to the yacht club under Sugar Loaf Mountain to see if any boats were for sale. We immediately found a 40 foot wooden hulk with a blown engine with a "For Sale" sign on it. The owner was an airline pilot for **Varig Airlines**, and thank god he had a conscience for after we had met with him several times and Nora's dad, an experienced sailor, was getting ready to fly down for the trip, the pilot called and backed out, telling us in brutal honesty that the boat was rotten to the water line.

In the meantime, most of the twenty or so members of our original training group would usually go out to a different, exciting restaurant each evening. This was the only time in Peace Corps that I actually had a little money. My so called Peace Corps savings, meant for me to re-acclimate back into society, allowed me a heady repast from poverty. Oddly, this would be about the only time during the rest of my life, with the exception of the last few years, that I wasn't living at the bottom of the poverty chart. For two to three dollars American, at the most, we would eat out at the finest restaurants in Rio. Suffice to say we had a blast at seafood palaces where every sea creature except Moby Dick was displayed in the iced-front windows, at an elaborate smorgasbord inside an enormous Viking ship or churrascorias, or at Brazilian steak houses with dozens of skewers holding meat over hot coals. Even in the elegant restaurants, they would bring you a spit of impaled meat, the procedure being to cut off the perfectly done golden brown on the outside before the waiter would come by and take it back to the coals. One of these meals usually involved having your spit put back on the coals three or four times while you ate and carved your meal with a dagger.

Our whole gang had to stay around Rio for a couple of extra days after Carnival because none of the banks would change dollars into cruzeiros, or vice-versa, since the cruzeiro was about to officially fall against the dollar. Inflation, in Brazil, was always over 100% per year, and this shutdown of the money exchanges was a regular occurrence. Then the adventurous group of five travelers-to-be decided to take off on a bus south to Uruguay and Argentina in route by train to Chile and then northward to the USA. As usual the buses were new Mercedes. Cathy (another lady from training) and I had slept together in those last exuberant days in Rio, so I was saying goodbye to three sweet things. A buddy from day one, a guidance counselor named Gene, looked at me in shock on the way to the money exchange the morning before he flew out to New York and the five of us took off south, "You're sleeping with three women?" Gene just kept shaking his head and looking over at me as we shared a cab to the embassy. NONE of the other men were being bothered by the draft while I knew they were close behind me now, so perhaps I was trying to leave my genes here on earth in case I was killed in war.

Peace Corps Syndrome

RUA FERREIRA VIANA, 71 A 81 · FLAMENGO · TEL. 45-8160
END. TELEG. FLORHOTEL · RIO DE JANEIRO - GB · BRASIL

23 de Fevereiro '68,

Hi,

Arrived, cashed my check, and am having a ball getting Sauteaued, Dancing Carnival, Partying. There are about 150 P.C.V.'s in town. All ready to Play. We start late, get in bed about 3, + sleep till 12:00. We're going in a few minutes. I just wanted to say Hello + that I'm really enjoying myself.

There were some good times on the bus ride south with Rob, Dan, Nora and Chris. I was such a horny little devil that soon Nora and I were cooing and rubbing different body parts as we began the mountainous part of the trip. Horrifyingly, the driver would turn off his headlights as we raced around seemingly endless miles of "S" curves. The logic being that if other traffic was coming, the driver could see it. By using this logic the driver would take the inside lane on every one of the blind curves ahead. If there had been a stalled vehicle or anything on the other side of the road, we would have all died tumbling down the side of some very steep mountain roads. Somehow the idea that there might be another such vehicle without lights for the same reason never entered the minds of the driver. This was common practice. Maybe this was the excitement that spurred me and Nora into rubbing on each other as one by one the other passengers turned their lights off as did we.

Soon we were making several attempts at making a spoon, then Nora was riding my lap, first facing me and when those muscles spasmed out, we tried most of the other Kama Sutra positions before we stopped the show I'm sure several around us were quite aware of even though we were in pitch blackness.

Arriving in Montivideo, Uruguay, we soon found a great two bedroom suite in a marvelous old hotel of past glory, but still nice enough for us and unbelievably cheap. The rooms had giant windows that soared from the 12 foot ceilings down to the floor almost and tall glass doors that opened onto wide balconies overlooking the harbor. The Uruguayan National Casino caught our attention from the corner balcony and Rob exclaimed, "We ought to go win a million or two." I always thought Rob might have a million or two back home in Tennessee; he had the feel of old money and wasn't being bothered by the draft board like I was.

So off we went to the casino where we had a few drinks and bet and lost a couple of dollars. I'll never forget one of the decadent rich betting enormous sums at the roulette wheel, tens of thousands of dollars on every spin. With each spin he'd push several piles of these big oblong chips into the middle of the table. The windows we went to only had round chips... worth maybe up to a thousand US. The next day in Montivideo found us in the leather shops where I soon found myself being measured for a dark russet brown, suede jacket. I designed it on paper and had it made for about 40 bucks, big baggy pockets, belted, it was hot looking and perfect for traveling through the Andes.

The five of us strolled across the street from the leather shop to a restaurant above the bay for lunch. A fairly large main room opened onto a view of the ocean out back, and a big, round, cushioned booth drew us over like magnets. I wandered to the back glass doors to see a couple of old freighters anchored across an inlet off the bay and wound

Peace Corps Syndrome

up sitting on the outside of the red leathered booth. We were just beginning to suck on some cold beers when Rob nudged me into looking up the stairs as several foxy ladies, two of them black bombshells, came down the wide steps looking directly at us, moving their lips like they were in the throes of blatant pleasure. Boing! Rob bumped my shoulder again and said, "Jesus Christ, chocolate desert!" We were all completely accustomed to the presence of prostitutes since they were everywhere in Brazil, and I think most of us had worked with such ladies since they usually came to the Health Posts where we worked to get their required health cards.

   The hottest of the two black girls and a blonde walked over and started talking and flirting with our group. We offered to buy a couple of beers for the two when they asked us if we'd buy them a Cerveja. Since I was on the outside of the booth, the mahogany-brown-black, Nubian goddess with a delicious smile made room for herself, and I soon found myself being rubbed on with her gorgeous dark brown breast falling out of her blouse onto my shoulder. I had no choice but to nod and almost giggle as did the group when she asked if any of us would like to go upstairs to dance the "Watusi." Pat, my Peace Corps girl friend in 67, was a northern Michigan, full bloodied Indian, and I'd slept with one of the Brazilian agricultural reps back in Fatima do Sul just after I arrived, a neat little Japanese bundle. We bounded up the stairs to a cute, nice sized room with lots of mirrors and classic eight foot windows. We undressed in a flash and as she lay down and spread her legs; I was amazed as I saw my first black pussy, beautiful rosy pink petals highlighted by the absolute ebony of her bush and that beautiful dark healthy brown just short of black of her gorgeous body. I'll never forget how she girl giggled as I ate her rosy oyster just above the waters of Montivideo's harbor until she started trying to pull my ears off, moaning like she was calling banshees as she had her first orgasm. I could smell the heady aroma of her and the backwaters of the bay, a delightful blend, see seagulls and hear them as I looked up into the huge mirror behind the bed just as I climbed up and on top of her, pulling her long nipples up 4 or 5 inches with my lips as I planted my white southern flag and rode her across time, the Selma bridge and through the racism of my Southern heritage. (My great-uncle, Dwight Shaw, had been foreman of U.S. Pipe and Foundry back in the 1917 Era and had killed the black leader of a striking group of blacks who were merely trying to get equal pay. Dwight beat the man to death with his bare hands and was considered a hero in Bessemer, Alabama where I grew up.)

My ebony goddess and I both came at the same time, sweating in that sexual southern slipperyness that people that grew up with air conditioning will never enjoy. I stayed on top for a minute or so giving her nipple a slow suckle as I erased decades of racism and shot off into her pulsating pink pussy. Now, I felt I was truly not a racist having slept with every race of women on earth. I was a straight laced kid from Alabama who had never gone to school or church or ever even had a real conversation with a black person until Peace Corps. I was a kid who innocently went to see Peter, Paul and Mary and Joan Baez outside Montgomery, Alabama the night before the Selma marchers were to enter the capital; was refused service at a restaurant on the way home suspected, no doubt, of being an agitator, state troopers glaring at us; a kid who would have been expelled the very next day from a state school, Alabama College, if the administration found out that we had attended the music show in Montgomery; a kid who suddenly found himself at Miles College, an all black school in Birmingham to see and hear Joan Baez in the school's chapel; singing along with the rest in the auditorium in the recording of "We Shall Overcome." This was the famous version that appeared on her album, and I think on a single that was played worldwide for decades,

Peace Corps Syndrome

inadvertently making me an international-singing-civil-rights-activist. I had overcome!

The next day in Montivideo found our quintet on the shore of a wide body of water boarding a 100 passenger hydrofoil monster of a boat that would take us across the Rio de la Plata to Buenos Aires. The ride was fairly uneventful as the boat idled out of the inlet while attendants made sure that we were buckled into our seats. Out in the open waters the hydrofoil suddenly turned into a very noisy monster as the huge thruster engines began to rev-up. Soon we rose up about 10 feet higher off the water than we had been and began this horrible, tooth-jarring nightmare of a ride so rough that it soon became almost intolerable.

Rob and I were sitting beside the door that went up on deck, and finally he looked over and nodded toward the door. We sneaked out of our seats and soon were on top of the bucking monster beast at a spot about 20 feet behind the ship's cockpit, a living room sized area surrounded on all sides by windows. From our vantage point we could watch three people, the pilots, all apparently quite involved in steering and throttling the giant Pteryadactyl-like beast trying to escape the bonds of water as it thundered across the miles and miles of the Rio de la Plata. Finally one of the pilot's head turned and he saw us hanging onto the aft deck by our fingernails and started gesturing frantically for us to go below.

Our shaken group emerged on the shores of Argentina where we took a bus into Buenos Aires and disembarking downtown soon found a hotel referred to us by other PCV'S, another national treasure of two hundred year old architecture which meant big suites at low prices split five ways. Buenos Aires was famous for its sweaters, its woolens and alpaca products. We all went shopping, and I bought some beautiful alpaca pullovers for my mom and sister. But Rob was getting miserable about a Brazilian girl.

Back in Rio, Rob had been dating a gorgeous creature, a

recently divorced psychiatrist of all things, and I had just met her best friend, oddly enough, another recently divorced thirty-year-old psychiatrist but with a child. By the time we spent a few days visiting Buenos Aires, we had walked the city and talked to people our age who all seemed ready for the next revolution which sounded like it was going to happen the very next day, eaten at the best steak houses in the world and walked her unbelievably well planned boulevards as wide as Texas. Using an ancient five foot brass telescope set up alongside the Avenidas in the light of a full moon, I looked through a telescope for the very first time and wowed my brain examining the lunar craters floating above the surreally wide avenues.

I think the moon got to Rob because suddenly he was talking about going back to Rio instead of taking the trains across Argentina to Chile and home. I jumped at the chance to go back to Ipanema and Copa Cabana beaches. Roberta had a great four or five bedroom apartment two blocks off the beach in Ipanema with two live in maids. After some sad farewells to Nora, Dan and Chris, Rob and I were soon enduring another neck wrenching, tooth jarring nightmare ride across the miles and miles of the mighty Rio Plata.

That first night back in Rio found me set up again with Roberta's best friend, Lara, the other psychiatrist, at a gathering of six or eight of their friends, all with medical careers. We had plenty to talk about except that people from Rio, called Cariocas, talked with their own particular slang that I simply couldn't savvy a lot of, which they delighted in demonstrating. Rob's Brazilian was a million times better than mine; he had hung out with the daughter of the governor of Manaus and had a more educated bunch to talk with than my dear, sweet, "redneck," backwoods Brazilians.

Rob and Roberta were cuter together than three puppies and a kitten and they spent a lot of time in bed. Roberta

Peace Corps Syndrome

worked each day while Rob and I slept in. When we finally got up, the two cute little maids would bring in espressos and after a while ask if we wanted melon or toast and butter. Oh those Cariocan breakfasts on the balcony looking down three floors upon a street vegetable market that the maids frequented every day that went around all four sides of a small block. Sea breezes made thermals rise just behind and above us on the coastal mountains and by this time every day the squadrons of hundreds of black buzzards would begin their afternoon soaring contests. After the third espresso coffee at anywhere from 10:30 till noon, we would walk down past the vegetable stands toward the beach for a swim. There dozens of good looking girls, truly in little bitty bikinis covering very little, volley-balled and rubbed sun tan lotion on each other. We drooled all the way across our stroll on Ipanema, which like Rio's other beaches curve around the slopes of green mountains forming wide crescents of wealthy Brazilians at work and play. Their money was made back in the interior at giant cattle ranches that most had in their families. "Let your cattle do your working" to the tune of the yellow pages' ditty was quite appropriate.

As Rob and I sunned and played in the edges of the ocean, vendors would come along, some with big baskets or the five gallon, square tin cans that olive oil came in on top of their heads full of pineapples. If you wanted one, the vendor would take his machete and while holding the top whack off the sides, seemingly whacking away at his own hand, and give you a perfectly fresh pineapple to save one from the effects of the sun. We'd get so stickied-up eating the delicious juicy thing that we just had to go jump into the water.

Lara and I became lovers right away, and I soon found myself over at her house, a little up the slopes of the coastal mountain. She had an oral fetish which was serious enough for a psychiatrist to look into, but which delighted me for a

Ron Horton

while.

It was during this time that I received the strangest and most mean spirited letter of my life from the old lady who ran the draft board in Bessemer. I had just written my Aunt Ann in Alabama as a sounding board and for advice. Ann was more like a sister since she, her twin, Clara, and I had grown up together. Their father had committed suicide days before WW II had started out of cowardice to avoid some probable jail time for using WPA workers under his supervision in the family garden at 416 South Seventh Street in Bessemer, Alabama. They were only seven when I was born in the middle of the war and being the first grandbaby in the entire Walker family, they practically raised me. Nanny refused to teach the twins how to do ANY household chores and scraped together every dime her severely rheumatoid arthritic knee would allow her to earn working in clothing stores to send them to charm and modeling school in Birmingham. Ann's very first job was secretary to the president of the biggest bank in Alabama.

July, 1968
Dear Aunt Ann,
What a crazy mixed up world. I'm at a point in my life where I have to decide many things within a short period of two or three weeks. I've written Mother on this but I didn't care to alarm her with my (as usual) thoughts. I'm fairly certain how you'll react, but I decided to use you to get this off my chest, to get it on paper to help clear up my thoughts, and because I'd like your opinions. The whole problem as you know is the "draft." If I come home, there is one possibility only, and that is teaching (high school), which could be difficult so close to the opening of schools and due to the lack of a teaching diploma. If I didn't obtain a position, I believe my chances of being drafted to be at least 90%. On the same thought, I don't want to teach and doing so on a provisional certificate pays about $3,700,

Peace Corps Syndrome

which is semi-poverty. I am staying with a businessman in Sao Paulo at the moment, who has offered (I wrote you, but letters aren't getting out of Mato Grosso for us these days) me a very attractive position. One in which I would never make less than you are making and with the possibilities for the U.S. ingenuity to make 2-4 times of my dear Aunt's salary. I believe it possible to enter into the firm through my own efforts here and/or with a few American dollars (I'm speaking of from 1-3 years from now). The firm is in the wakening up stage and now is the perfect time to get into something that could, and will be a big thing. I don't know if this is repetition due to what you and Mother are writing about not receiving my letters. I've helped these people for about two months, and have seen how organization is lacking in the construction phases, and how this could be the key to enter in with them and step up production without more outlay of capital using that U.S. ingenuity I spoke of. Let me interject to say that as most P.C. volunteers at this hour of departure, I'm feeling regrets about leaving Brazil, and I'm afraid of returning to the normalcy of U.S. life, and the dread of becoming middle class, married, with three kids and bills. Brazil is like the U.S. was in the 1920's, i.e. prime for speculation and where it more than compensates to work here.

Well, back to the topics (if you can untangle all this). The time to enter into business is now not one year from now after having taught and reached the nondraftable age of 26. I'm seriously concerned with the thought of spending 2-3 years in the Armed Forces.

Out of all of this thought arrives almost utter confusion because of decisions that have to be made and things that will be happening within the next two weeks. To remain in Brazil (deferred) is an uncertainty due to lack of knowledge about appeals to the Board, i.e. if it can be done from here, there are several escapes. A request from the Brazilian Government that I'm useful to the socio-economic element (I'll write more on this when I know the letters are getting through) and/or marriage to an attractive friend (who understands all this) on an arbitrary basis of one year (to the age of 26), and possibly the loss of my left ring finger due to stiffness resulting from two breaks (this is between you and me). This is all out in left field, I know, but what are the solutions if not these to apply to the problems at the moment.

Only people like you and Calloway, and quick (drastic) thinkers get ahead. All of this is so god damn unreal it shakes me, your nephew in Brazil, single or married on this basis, or in Viet Nam, or the 10 % possibility of safety.

So somehow, I'm not going in the service; I'm going to work for a short period at home to by a car, and I'm going to work and invest here in Brazil. If I can avoid the draft, I want to buy a Corvette, and return in June; but we'll have plenty of time to talk about that later.

It'll be a little hard to readjust when I get home, so ignore me if I appear strange. I want to spend a few days at home, and then I have to get on top of things (draft board, teaching, etc.) Much love; I'll be arriving the 3rd week of August, I think, depending on how things go. Well, that's almost all so I'll close.

Love,
Ron

Peace Corps Syndrome

August 5, 1968

Hey Sweety,
Was delighted to receive your lenthy epistle yesterday, although some of its contents were somewhat disturbing to me. I can, therefore, well understand the tumultuous state you find yourself in at this point. I have given much thought (profound?) to the various points you raised, and if you will bear with me, I shall ramble on with some of my thinking.

First, I think that at this age and stage of your life, with no real responsibilities to speak of, you should do what will make you the happiest. The business opportunities there do sound limitless, and being in the right place at the right time is half of the battle. On the other hand, Ronnie, whatever your absence of two years has led you to believe, there is still no land for opportunities like the good old U.S.A. It is still—and will remain—the most bountiful, richest, and soundest economy in the world. While the opportunities are here, it will take the same commodity to success that it will take there—good old U.U. ingenuity.

Ron Horton

Sam and I often discuss the subject of business and success, and we have one common conclusion, and that is that most people are so lacking in the thought processes necessary to formulate a program, carry it successfully to its conclusion, and utilize some of the God-given mental powers we possess, that it is really unbelievable how nil the competition is for someone who is intelligent and aggressive. While teaching school is an honorable profession, I cannot fathom your reasoning that it is the only occupation available to you should you decide to come home. The benefit of your college education would enable you to go into any field you wished, merely with the proper amount of desire. If your opportunity there lies in the field of selling, I might also point out that the American salesman is the highest paid professional in the world today. Many of the large corporations only interview college graduates, as you well know, for these positions, and the market for heavy equipment here must vastly overshadow that of Brazil.

I know the draft is causing much of your present thinking. As an American citizen in Brazil, would you not be as subject to the draft living in Brazil as you would be living in Bessemer? I believe so. Certainly, you are not thinking of renouncing your American citizenship for any reason whatsoever. As you know much better than I, the South American (most, if not all) countries have never had a stable nor a sound economy nor government. At one time, Havana was a bonanza for most American businesses and millions were made there. With the overthrow of the government after the revolution, billions and billions of American dollars went down the drain. I am aware that you actually know much more about all of this than do I, but I am merely commenting on the various facets in case you have not considered both sides of the picture. Would your staying in Brazil exempt you from the American draft?

Peace Corps Syndrome

Would not a teaching positon here for the duration of one year be a safer bet? I have talked with a Marine Colonel here about getting you the next opening in the Reserve Unit; Robin has also been working on getting you in his Army Reserve unit. This involves one weekend a month for about 6 years, instead of 4 years in the Army on regular duty. Mr. Cothran's son, Bill, got into the Air National Guard, served 6 months, active, and is now back at Vanderbilt. There are answers other than active duty, admittedly it takes pull to get an opening in any of these. But we have all been working in your behalf, should you wish to go this route. If you could get into a reserve unit, you could go into any occupation you wished and forget the teaching if that isn't what you wish to do

Insofar as your regrets about leaving Brazil, I understand as I felt the same regrets about leaving Germany. I loved it and loved every moment I was there; should you decide to stay, I will also understand it as Clara and I would have done the same except for a veto from Nanny. But, at the risk of sounding as if I am waving the flag, there is still nothing like the States! I think we tend to forget life here after we have been away for as long as two years. Whether you live here, in Brazil, or in Spain, your life is just as routine and humdrum as you care to make it or just as lively and fun as you wish. People are people everywhere and most of our pleasures and enjoyment in life are derived from them in one form or another. Birmingham is not dull and life here simply is not drab— like anything else, you get out of it exactly what you put into it and nothing more. I think your capabilities and potential far exceed that of most people, and that you will do well regardless of where you are. Perhaps New York or the West Coast might appeal to you more. Perhaps I have the advantage of 7 years on you, Ronnie, but after having no one to care about that I cared about for so many years and in spite of the fun and excitement I have had with my

Ron Horton

care-free existence, there comes a time when "middle class, married and 3 kids and bills" sound much more appealing to you than you would believe. You can only drive one car at a time, sleep in one bed at a time, love one man or woman at a time, eat one meal at a time, regardless of your financial circumstances or station in life. The continuity of a meaningful relationship does not have to make it a dull existence.

Which brings me to your thinking of marriage (for a year?) to an attractive friend. Darling, that is a lifetime commitment (both moral and otherwise) and is not something to be used for a specific out for another problem such as the draft. If—and only If—you are in love with someone, I hope I can be the maid of honor, but you involve too many people and their lives whenever you do anything for any reason except the right one. It is even something worth waiting for if you do not find the real thing (I bet you think I sound like moonlight and roses, but it is what I really feel—from my vast experiences) as easily as some people seen to stumble into it. I was never that lucky, but I do know that right now I am thankful that I didn't compromise or "settle for" anything that I felt was less than what I really wanted and deserved.

I know you think I have tried to tear down your thinking, and I really have not. I just wanted you to know that the coin has two sides and you often have to look at both of them to get the whole picture. I personally feel your best bet is to come home, get into a reserve unit, and begin some American style of living. You may have forgotten how lovely, plush and nice life can be on this side of the ocean. If you decide to stay there, will you at least get to come home for a visit? I hope so.

Darling, I hope you understand even portions of the

Peace Corps Syndrome

thoughts I tried to convey in this letter. I appreciate your sharing yours with me, and I merely wanted to share with you how I honestly feel about the various subjects covered. I hope you already know that if you decide to stay over there, I will be happy with your decision and, always, under every circumstance only wish and hope you have the best. Some times facing realities is better than evading them, though, and I think it all makes us mere mortals stronger. I know your experiences there the past two years have had a marked effect on your personality, your character, and your whole life. I also know that you have done well and completed a job you set out to do. I think you can do this in any circumstance, for I have never had any doubts about you and your abilities. Whatever your decisions, know that my thoughts are with you. I will be most anxious to hear from you right away, so please write. More than anything, I hope we can look forward to seeing you before this month is over. In the meantime, take good care of yourself and I would not let anyone touch that finger without an expert medial opinion on it, preferably from a doctor here.

Til we see you hopefully soon, much love and kisses from your favorite ole maid Aunt! I'm hale, happy and hearty (still skinny) and hope I have helped your dilemma rather than added to it. Whatever makes you happy, will make me happy, I promise. I know your decision will be the right one, and I will be thinking about you. Let me hear!
Love,
Ann

It was at this time that I received a hateful little scrawled note (handwritten on the pages of a 1953 desk calendar) from my draft board. The exact wording of the letter follows for clarity.

Ron Horton

(Letter from Mary Lewis)

Sept. 13, 1968

From: Draft Board

This is in reference to your (sic.) received on this date-you are not eligible for any more deferment (sic.) as a student-inasmuch as you were not in school and had not completed a year in graduate school on or before Oct. 1967. As far as your being deferred as a teacher--it would have to be determined that replacing you as a teacher would cause loss of effectiveness in the school system and replacing you would be impossible. At our next scheduled board meeting you will be classified into Class A-1 and you will be order (sic.) for Armed Forces Physical Examination on our next call which will probably be in Oct. Failure to comply with this order will result in your being declared delinquent and ordered for immediate induction as a delinquent registrant. Your permit to depart from the U.S. has expired as of Aug. 68 and it is advisable for you to return as soon as possible. Please report to this local board upon your return immediately.

Mary S. Lewis
Exec. Sec.

The following pages contain the practically illegible note from my draft board written on scrap paper. They were not even civil enough to address me by name, but rather by my Social Security number.

Peace Corps Syndrome

Saturday, March 14, 1953

Sept 13

This is in reference to your received on this date — You are not eligible for any more deferment as a student — inasmuch as you were not in school & had not completed — yr. in graduate school on or before Oct 67 —

As far as your being deferred as a teacher — It

Sunday, March 15, 1953

would have to be determined that replacing you as a teacher would cause loss of effective ness to the school system & replacing you would be impossible.

At our next scheduled board meeting you will be reclassified into class 1A & you will be ordered for Armed

Monday, March 16, 1953

Force Physical Examination on our next call which will Probably be in Oct.

Failure to Comply with this Order will result in your being declared delinquent & ordered for immediate induction as a delinquent registrant.

Your permit to depart from the US has expired as of Aug 68 & it is advisable for

Peace Corps Syndrome

Tuesday, March 17, 1953

APPOINTMENTS

A.M.
8-30
9-00
9-30
10-00
10-30
11-00
11-30
12-00

P.M.
12-30
1-00
1-30
2-00
2-30
3-00
3-30
4-00
4-30
5-00
5-30

You to return as soon as possible. Please report to this local board upon your return immediately —

Mary S. Lein
Exo. Sec.

The petty little bureaucrats at the Selective Service office in my home town treated me like scum as I was exiting Peace Corps and returning to the country. "Don't you think it's time to serve your country?" they had said in one of their communications. What the hell did they think the Peace Corps was anyhow? None of the rich or connected kids were ever drafted; they were all in graduate school or the reserves. Anyone who was married or with two years of grad school was exempted. If I had not dropped out of grad school, I would have been exempt from the draft, but by going into Peace Corps, I had somehow made myself cannon fodder by listening to President John Kennedy, and when I had "Asked what I could do for my country," I had gotten screwed. That's what I could do for my country… ruin my damned life.

The threat of Viet Nam was so repulsive to me that I had been considering shooting off one of my fingers and had tried to find out if the hurt finger on my left hand from the Kombi accident would exempt me if I somehow inexplicably didn't have it any longer. The most serious thing that I actually did was trying to catch the really bad kind of malaria, the reoccurring kind called falciparum. I regularly did malaria exams at the Health Post when I was there or at different reservations and was rather expert at the time about the four types. Three of the four are temporary and go away but not Malaria falciparum; it never goes away and can come back at any time in your life so was a draft deferment, so I heard. I began to be on the lookout for cases of this type, even asking other labs if they had any cases as our lab hadn't seen any falciparum for a while.

Finally, one day at the Heath Post as I drew blood from a shaking 30-year-old guy with a cheap straw hat and home made sandals soled with car tires who complained of being cold in the 100 degree heat, I thought I might have a good possible. As soon as the slide was ready, I put in under my microscope and voila, falciparum. After questioning the slash and burn farmer about where he lived and where he might have caught it, I left the lab after my shift and

Peace Corps Syndrome

planned my expedition to go catch this horrible disease. Four or five times a week, for over a month, I'd ride my old swayback blue and green horse a couple of miles south toward where the farmer had been bitten by what I soon discovered to be some of the meanest mosquitoes on this earth. When I'd get close to his mud and stick house, I'd veer off down toward the creek about a hundred yards, get off my horse and find a fallen tree to sit on. Immediately the skeeters would start landing on my arms and face, but I didn't shake them off, instead I let them bite me over and over, day after day. Dozens of little red balloons inflating themselves with my blood...drink on and leave your parasite with me. I was trying to be sick for the rest of my life to escape the draft, but it wasn't to be.

I never caught the damned disease, so by the time Rob and I returned to Rio, I was really getting frantic. Finally, I began to ask the medical group we were partying with if they had any hepatitis patients I could infect myself with. They were highly sympathetic, but all refused to participate in what they saw as insanity, certainly none of these 5% controlling 95% had ever had anything comparable to worry about.

Rob and I were just beginning to talk about heading north to the States but through Belem on the Amazon, when another letter arrived from my Aunt Ann in Birmingham which changed everything. After a weekend of revelry with Roberta and the gang, on Monday morning Rob and I rode the bus up north on the beach boulevard through one of the mountain tunnels that make Rio's coast particularly intriguing to the Hotel Florida to check for mail from the States. I turned white as the sand on the beach when I read the note from my aunt, which simply said, "If you're not in Montgomery, Alabama on Wednesday morning, you'll be drafted whether you're here or not."

It was Monday morning, I had about $300; it took about

$550 to fly back through New York, and the next flight LEFT on Wednesday. I was screwed. There was a flight that day through Miami which cost a lot more than the New York route for some reason. My visa and passport were actually null and void... had been for several weeks. I couldn't stay in Brazil since you were checked for papers all over the country at every border, so I couldn't go to work for Antonio. Instantly Rob was ready to help, bless his heart, for many reasons, some that I'm just beginning to figure out forty years later. We instantly grabbed a cab; I don't remember saying goodbye to anyone such was my desperate haste. Possessed, I walked into the airport and up to the national airline desk, Rob just behind with all or most of our bags. I regret to this day leaving without addresses to Roberta...it happened so fast. The desk clerk of the Brazilian national airline, **VARIG,** looked up as this wild eyed maniac pretending to be me explained that if I wasn't back in the USA immediately I'd be in Viet Nam before Christmas, and I had only about HALF of what it cost for the ticket. I was always able to talk folks into doing things when I'm sincere.

The guy never blinked nor hesitated, simply said, "Olhe, nao tem problema" as he started filling in tickets to New York and Atlanta, explaining that was as far as he could get me for my $300 on the $750 airfare. He wrote and then scratched across several tickets, writing notes and stapling stuff together to cover his shenanigans. Wham, bam and we were lifting off the field heading toward Sugar Loaf Mountain again, only this time I was no green PCV, I was a hard ass cynic who felt like bureaucracy was about to kill him.

The inanity of it all weighed on me, yet the plane continued to rise, the gentle curves of Copacabana and Ipanema off to my right as was Antonio a thousand miles inland and what turned out to be the most lucrative opportunity of my life, all vanishing out of sight as the

Peace Corps Syndrome

plane banked to the left and turned out to sea before heading north by northwest to New York. Crashing into Sugar Loaf Mountain held no fear for me now that I had skimmed whole mountain ranges in dense clouds flying out of the Rockefeller Ranch. That Wednesday morning in Montgomery, if I made it or not, I would be drafted and sent to Viet Nam. But finally, I was heading toward the Amazon, just as Peace Corps had promised me two-and-a half years before, only just like last time I was going to be 35,000 feet above it. The overwhelming sense of betrayal, the sheer unfairness of it all left me wide eyed like a trauma patient.

The flight back was uneventful. I remember Rob sitting beside me, but that's all. We landed in New York at midmorning on Tuesday; I had passage to Atlanta but that wasn't Birmingham or Montgomery. I had only about 18 hours left before I'd be drafted and AWOL. Brazenly I walked up to the **Varig** desk, and my eyes must have told the horrible truth better than my words as I once again told my story. Once again came those almost exact words, "Hey man…no problem." Taking my pile of tickets he began the same game the desk agent in Rio had played, scrawling and stapling. He soon handed me tickets to Atlanta and Birmingham. The fact that two miracles had occurred didn't dawn on me, nor did the third miracle that happened Wednesday morning.

Years later as I wrote this, I wondered for the first time if Rob hadn't been standing behind me the whole time waving the rest of my fare to the agents, but surely I would have seen that even in my state. It was only later that I wondered about Rob and the medical group in Rio coming up with something that Rob could slip me in a drink that caused the third miracle. We flew together to Atlanta, though it's so vague now I barely remember saying goodbye, such was my condition as we landed. I took off almost immediately for Birmingham while he was going home to Memphis. I called mom from Atlanta, and when I landed in Birmingham Tuesday night half my family was waiting for me at the airport.

I had to be at the draft board at 6:30 the next morning for the bus ride to Montgomery, a really horrible two hour nightmare, I thought, into the jungles of Asian warfare. The physicals were the most demeaning thing that I have ever been through, even divorce court. Naked we shuffled along the various lines to be poked, probed, testicle tickled while we coughed, and to finally pee into a cup. The nightmare continued on the bus ride back to Bessemer. It wasn't until Friday that I received notice that I had failed my physical, albumin in my urine. I actually had no idea what that meant, urinalysis was never in my training nor practice while working in a lab. The letter said that I had a six month deferment, during which time I had to have a complete urinalysis done locally. A miracle…a reprieve! It was by now a week since the local schools had started, but there were still unfilled positions I discovered in Birmingham and Mobile. Teaching would keep me out of the army and Viet Nam. It really was a miracle.

I decided to take the job in Mobile because it was on the coast and several old friends from Alabama College were living there. I was hired to teach biology at Vigor High School but immediately the butt ugly monster of stupidity and bureaucracy reared its head and grabbed my gonads in its poisonous maw. Vigor was the biggest white redneck high school in Mobile and had been forced to integrate only two weeks before I arrived and riots and fights had occurred every day. The principal on signing my draft deferment form had turned to his secretary and had her issue the memo, "Do you have any students you would like to give to our new Alabama history and social studies teacher?" I was given 175 problem kids, the worst behavior problems, all the fighters, the meanest, the most

Peace Corps Syndrome

bigoted of each race, now together 35 to 40 at a time in my classes.

I made only about $3500 dollars a year, enough for a shack on the river and payments on a VW. I remember days when I literally only had white flour to eat, no oil even to cook it, just water and white flour cooked in an old aluminum pot with no oil. As it cooked I had to beat the pot in an upside down position to get it out and eat the cardboard like crap. Great profession! I managed to make the kids like me somehow and actually taught a little, but when at the end of the school year a call went out for volunteers for the former all black high school across the tracks by the paper mill, I immediately volunteered at the chance to teach Earth Science.

I made some great friends at Mobile County Training School as it was called. The school sat only two hundred yards from the paper mill and the pollution was so great that unless you availed yourself of the use of the free car washes at the mill, the gummy pollution would build up to the point where it was simply irremovable from your car's finish. You couldn't wash out your lungs, however. The last slave auction block in Alabama was here in Plateau and many of the black teachers felt like they had been sold down the river once again when their high school was turned into the junior high! Just two years before, two members of County's championship baseball team had gone to the majors. The New York Mets, I think; Tommy Agee and Cleon Jones are still heroes in Mobile as they were in the 1967 World Series. My neighbor down the hall, Spencer Merriweather, was the no nonsense art teacher in what was the integrated junior high school; he immediately adopted me as his best friend as I did him. There was only one other white teacher and two questionably white students. I'll never forget the five foot white lady tearing after a miscreant across the school lawn, tackling him, and taking him to the office.

Ron Horton

Somehow the principal didn't know what giving the finger was when I took a ninth grade girl to his office. The girl had been giving me the finger every day in the hall just before running around the corner. I was wearing a little woven, dyed rawhide Brazilian Indian bracelet that I had to soak to stretch to get on my wrist. Many of the boys in the school were much larger than I was and on several occasions walked into my room saying they were there to kill the white son-of-a-bitch teacher. That first year at Vigor when racial riots or fights happened, all the teachers and the administration would disappear; only an enormous three hundred and seventy pound coach and I would wade in to break the fights up.

My guardian angels were doing overtime those years. Spencer passed word to all his classes that my leather bracelet was an award as the highest karate honor, so I guess the two or three, two hundred pounders I had to take to the office each week with their arm twisted behind their back were fewer in number because of Spencer. I relished my days there at first, going off with Spencer after school to a bar over by another black school where we'd drink some kind of flavored stuff I've never seen since... great times though and soon I was helping him coach Pee Wee football. The players were so small and young that we chuckled a great deal of the time at their antics. A typical occurrence was like the time on kickoff when the three foot tall kicker kicked the ball over his head and backwards fifteen yards or so. Ole Merriweather and I rolled on the ground for a long time before reassuring the youngsters to do it again.

Weekends would find me at one of the all black clubs; the worse dive in Prichard had a restroom you couldn't get within 20 feet of but hosted B.B. King, Bobby Bluebland and others. I never saw another white person there, but I was always treated just like one of the gang; I loved it. Some new friends opened the chicest supper club in town

Peace Corps Syndrome

in a massive antebellum mansion. What a contrast.

The shit hit the fan at the end of my second year back from Brazil when after final exams the 20% or so of my students who couldn't or wouldn't study received F's, and the principal went berserk. Whenever I walked into the office, he would be inspired to start screaming at me; two years teaching, two asshole principals and bureaucrats. When I returned at the start of the next school year, I was assigned to teach NEW MATH, whatever the hell that was, and the math teacher next door, who somehow had also pissed off the principal, was assigned to teach history. I had a triple major at Alabama College and one was in history, but the principal wouldn't change our assignments.

That first summer I worked 80 hours a week running a Pizza Hut in Mobile, and the next year setting my pay up on a twelve month system made getting by even harder since it made my take home under a hundred and fifty dollars per month. I found an old paperback thirty years later where I had written my monthly budget down for that first year: after taxes and the seventy five dollar car payment was taken out of my paycheck, I had $175 to live on. Now I had even less. It was just as bad as or worse than my living standard in Peace Corps. I remember talking a filling station guy into giving me money on my gas credit card each month to live on. I never broke out of the poverty trap that Peace Corps had snared me with for the rest of my life.

During the fall there had been a National Draft Lottery and numbers were assigned to all of us Viet Nam fodder. Miraculously, I had a real high number. I would not be drafted, so one day in the middle of the second year at County, I just didn't go back. I quit the moment that I had enough of the system. But I had no money and could not even consider going back to Brazil and Antonio. Hell, airfare and traveling expenses was half of what I made a year.

Ron Horton

It took me a quarter of a century to figure out exactly what Peace Corps had really done to me, The Syndrome. After teaching I put on my suit and became a clothing buyer for an enormous department store and became their boy wonder, working seventy hours a week and partying with all the big shots at Gayfer's Store for the three months I gave my entire life to them. They started me out at about five thousand a year promising me big raises as I progressed. I figured that after my ninety-day trial period they'd really bump me up in salary, so when the moment came and the hundred-thousand-dollar-a-year store manager congratulated me for my marvelous work and announced my raise was fifteen dollars a week, I looked him in the eye and said, "I want all my back overtime. I quit and fuck you!"

Within weeks I had opened a red beans and rice/coffee house by the new University of South Alabama, and since my friends were the first "hippies" in Mobile found my joint to be the hangout for intellectual discussion. Opening night was tremendous…oodles of homemade baked goods by gorgeous ladies, marijuana brownies under the counter for friends. Several other old friends, oddly also the first white teachers in all black schools in Mobile, had become as disillusioned as fast as I had and also resigned in midyear (both white and black school administrators in those first years of integration were intent on making it NOT work), so I soon found about fifteen people living in my house at 808 Cody Road or out back in campers and tents.

Mr. Natural's was the name of my coffeehouse which I soon gave to the group as a source of income. I had a black neighbor with a tractor plant about an acre in garden vegetables. **Mr. Natural's** was outside the city and when I went to the courthouse for a vegetable curb market permit, I was amazed to be turned down. Bureaucracy strikes again it seemed, but I understood it all when some real nice

Peace Corps Syndrome

policemen stopped by to warn us about the giant group of evangelicals who had a church and school complex just past my place. The cops said the group was talking about burning us out and had put pressure on the county to get rid of us.

Some mutual friends had just visited the Ozarks and came by telling about land at twenty-five bucks an acre, so within weeks we were in Eureka Springs, Arkansas and living on land actually given to us on arrival, so magic was the genteel nature of our commune. Soon there were three teepees, and I was going barefoot, wearing a loincloth and rising at dawn as the sun came into my eastward facing teepee opening to go jump into the pond at first light and thank the spirits for the day. In the woods around us were hundreds of similar folk, arriving as we did, escaping the stupidity of Nixon and Spiro Agnew's attempt to rob us of the freedom of speech; just as GW, Cheney and Rumsfield are doing as I finish this book. Fuck all of 'em!

I always felt guilty after Peace Corps about having any material comfort. That is the most overwhelming part of Peace Corps Syndrome. I left the commune the next year and over the next few years spent a year living in a cave outside Eureka; it did have ten half-glass/half-wood doors under the overhang to cut off most of the wind....four years in different tents. One big army tent had real ornate Victorian gingerbread around it and a sleeping loft, but in winter time I still woke up with ice in my beard and moustache. Later when I went back to graduate school in order to fulfill my lifelong dream of teaching university biology, I was so broke I had to spend two more years in the Ozarks without heat, more ice every morning in my moustache. On real cold mornings the two would freeze together, and I would have to rub the icy hairs back and forth in order to open my mouth.

Six years of graduate school and three years teaching at the University where I had been a pre-Peace Corps kid found me laid-off and bankrupt because of an asshole of a dean who lowered my twenty-thousand-a-year salary without telling me and forced me over the edge into bankruptcy. When the state cut funds to universities in Alabama in the mid-nineties I was out on the street, worn out from years of construction jobs, no income, no future. If I had gone straight into graduate school back in the sixties and hadn't answered JFK's call to Peace Corps, I could have been teaching biology at some university and driving an antique MG with a neat little button down tweed cap.

When Social Security sent me my lifetime earnings in 2001, I had been working since 1959, all the way through high school; in fact, I had worked forty hours a week my last semester in high school, years and years of construction, six years as a public school teacher, and my earnings came to less than a doctor I knew in Fairhope, Alabama who specialized in pain and made three million a year made in a month. That is what Peace Corps syndrome is all about.

CPSIA information can be obtained at www.ICGtesting.com
Printed in the USA
LVOW041808300113

317938LV00002B/322/A